Enjoying Retirement

MICHAEL LONGHURST

Enjoying Retirement

An Australian handbook of ideas, strategies and resources

hachette
AUSTRALIA

IMPORTANT NOTE TO READERS
Although every effort has been made to ensure that the contents of this book are accurate, it must not be treated as a substitute for professional consultation. Always consult a qualified practitioner in the relevant field. Neither the author nor the publisher can be held responsible for any loss or claim arising out of the use, or misuse, of the suggestions made or the failure to take advice.

hachette AUSTRALIA

This edition published in Australia and New Zealand in 2018
by Hachette Australia
(an imprint of Hachette Australia Pty Limited)
Level 17, 207 Kent Street, Sydney NSW 2000
www.hachette.com.au

First published by Hodder Headline Australia Pty Limited in 2000 as *The Beginner's Guide to Retirement*

NATIONAL LIBRARY OF AUSTRALIA

A catalogue record for this book is available from the National Library of Australia

ISBN: 978 0 7336 3982 1 (paperback)

Cover design by Luke Causby, Blue Cork
Cover photographs courtesy of Getty Images and AdobeStock
Author photograph courtesy of Bill Griffiths
Text design by Bookhouse, Sydney
Typeset in 12/16.4 pt Simoncini Garamond by Bookhouse, Sydney
Printed and bound in Australia by McPherson's Printing Group

MIX
Paper from responsible sources
FSC® C001695
FSC www.fsc.org

The paper this book is printed on is certified against the Forest Stewardship Council® Standards. McPherson's Printing Group holds FSC® chain of custody certification SA-COC-005379. FSC® promotes environmentally responsible, socially beneficial and economically viable management of the world's forests.

To Paul, for the music and his unswerving adherence to what is right.

To June, who taught Mandy and I to believe in ourselves by celebrating our successes.

You are beginning a glorious opportunity to learn – to give new things a go – be prepared to use your talents – use all of your abilities to widen your lifestyle – try everything until you are satisfied.

Contents

Preface

Some years ago, when I was planning my own retirement from life as an organisational psychologist, I was hearing stories about people who thrived in retirement as well as sad examples of those who found retirement to be a stressful, even boring experience. As a psychologist and potential retiree, I was keen to find out why these differences occurred. I therefore enrolled in a Master's degree by research at Monash University in Melbourne in order to provide some rigour to the research – the *Retire 200* project was the result, and much of this book is based on its findings.

As the research progressed, it became apparent that most of the areas causing problems for people in retirement could be managed or removed through counselling or through the application of behavioural strategies, even where individuals had been retired for some years. It was this factor, combined with the encouragement of many of the participants of the *Retire 200* program, that led to the writing of the first edition of this self-help book.

Since that time, I have run countless seminars and workshops, and have delivered main platform speeches to thousands of retirees.

As I meet with the attendees of these sessions, their feedback confirms that the initial research findings remain as valid today as they were when the research was first conducted. What has changed, however, is the range of activities that are now available and which help facilitate social interaction among other like-minded people. Some prominent examples include social groups such as Meetup and The Australian Men's Shed Association. These groups and others are discussed later in this book.

How to use this book

Each chapter of the book deals with a separate topic and is completely self-contained. It is therefore possible to go straight to the chapters that interest you most and to work your way through them. The descriptions of processes required to modify entrenched behaviours are in a format that is clear and that can be applied to an individual's personal situation. Consequently, the style sometimes resembles that of a psychological text or instruction manual. As one reviewer of the book put it, 'This book needs to be read and *then* studied!'

Layout of the book

The introductory chapter of the book differs from all the other chapters in that it is dedicated to reporting the research findings of the *Retire 200* program. There is also a brief description of the research design process for those who are interested in such matters.

The remaining chapters address subjects that have been found to impact the happiness or otherwise of people in retirement. Each of these chapters follows the same convention, namely:

- The retirement-related issue (staying active, dealing with depression etc.) is discussed in the light of research findings of the *Retire 200* research program and of other recent social research.
- Practical methods for addressing the issues are then suggested.

Throughout the chapters appear quotes from participants of the *Retire 200* program so that you may see yourself in their words and be guided by their advice.

I hope you enjoy the book and find it helpful. Your observations and suggestions for improvement or addition are welcomed. I can be contacted at P.O. Box 305 Tewantin, Queensland, 4565, by email at: mike_longhurst@yahoo.com or at enjoyingretirement.net

Mike Longhurst
Retired Consulting Psychologist

INTRODUCTION

The findings of the *Retire 200* program – research with 200 Australian retirees

Some people thrive in retirement. Each day brings new joys and new adventures, with retirement being one of the happiest times of their lives. It is the time when the responsibilities of raising families have ended, when mortgages have been paid, and when it is *their* time to do their own thing.

For others, however, retirement can be a time beset with depression, fear, anxiety, and a sense of futility. It is as if all meaningful life has ended, and boredom has become the emotion of the day.

What are the differences between these two groups of people? More importantly, what do happy people do in retirement that unhappy people do not?

What to do in retirement

There are many factors that most of us can *guess* impact on satisfaction with retirement. For example, what sort of activities do people choose when they have retired? Do they sit around reading all the books they had wanted to read when they were too busy? Do they involve themselves in activities such as sport or voluntary work? Is doing all the fishing one has dreamt of doing the way to go, or is it better to lead a life with more structure and challenges?

Why did we retire?

In addition to what we *do*, it has long been thought that the circumstances surrounding *why* we retired have a significant impact on our emotional wellbeing. Did we retire of our own free will, or were we pushed into retirement by forces outside of our control? How long does it take us to deal with the transition from full-time work?

How do we remain physically and emotionally well?

Have we thought about how we are going to maintain our levels of fitness and mobility as we grow older? Will 'having too much time on our hands' lead to problems such as loneliness, depression or substance abuse?

What happens if we do not have enough money?

Given that even modest lifestyles require income, will we have sufficient money to enjoy our retirement? Having to watch every cent we spend so that we have enough money for food and shelter does not seem fair when we have worked hard all our lives. Yet, if provision is not made for retirement through superannuation or personal investments, such a lifestyle is a possible outcome.

Finding the answers through research

The objective of the research program was to build on earlier research from the United States and Australia to answer the above questions, and to identify the behaviours that differentiated well-adjusted retirees from their less happy peers. Having identified the behaviours of well-adjusted retirees, other retirees could then consider adapting their own behaviour to improve their satisfaction with life.

Who were the people on the *Retire 200* research project?

The sample of retired people studied in the research comprised 100 men and 100 women drawn from rural and urban areas of each Australian state, and from a cross-section of pre-retirement occupations. Participants in the program were volunteers who were recruited to the research via radio and the print media, and from notices on bulletin boards of retirement organisations.

The *Retire 200* research process

Designing effective social research is a complicated process. For example, if the research had comprised male retirees only, you would expect to get a one-sided view of what life in retirement is really like. As most retired couples will tell you, the roles of husband and wife often change considerably after retirement – any researcher who sought the views of just one gender would almost certainly miss the full picture. Unfortunately, much of the past research has focused on the male view of life in retirement and consequently has tended to present an incomplete view of retirement reality.

It is also important to ensure that the people being studied do not come from the same geographical area, or from similar incomes or occupations. If people across the general public are to draw meaningful conclusions that they can apply to their own lives, it is important that those participating in the research also comprise a representative sample of society.

Differentiating those who were well adjusted to retirement from those who were not

As we mentioned earlier, the aim of the research was to identify behaviours that differentiated those participants on the program who had adjusted well to retirement, from those for whom retirement was a less happy experience. The degree to which a participant was regarded as 'well adjusted' to retirement was based on a combination of the following indicators:

(i) Their levels of retirement-related anxiety.
(ii) Their levels of retirement-related depression.
(iii) Their levels of retirement-related stress.
(iv) Their levels of 'comparative global satisfaction' – that is, their satisfaction with life in retirement when compared with life before retirement.

The eight major findings from the *Retire 200* project

Eight areas were found to impact significantly on the degree to which participants adjusted satisfactorily to retirement.

1. Being able to retire of your own free will.
2. Being able to retire at age fifty-five or younger.
3. Being financially independent.
4. Engaging in 'Purposeful Activities' for more than five hours per week.
5. Having someone on whom you could rely for emotional support.

6. Proactively maintaining your health through exercise, diet, and regular medical check-ups.
7. Planning for retirement – both financially and for an active lifestyle.
8. Receiving pre-retirement advice or education.

We will now look closer at what each of these findings mean for those who have retired or who are about to retire.

Research Finding One: Being able to retire of your own free will – *'Jumping versus being pushed'*

The attitude with which we approach retirement usually relates to the degree to which we can control how and when we retire. Even when everything goes the way we plan it, the decision-making period is usually a stressful and emotional time. It can also be a frightening time for those close to the retired person, who may worry about how the changed circumstances will affect all concerned.

Retrenchment

We often see stories in the media about the effects of organisational mergers and downsizing. Most of these stories focus on the immediate financial hardships experienced by those who have been retrenched, and on their efforts to regain employment. However, for many older people, retrenchment also means involuntary retirement, and there is little doubt that many of those whose life plans are interrupted by forced retirement carry the effects of their pain well into retirement.

During the research program, a man was interviewed who had been retrenched from his job at the age of sixty-one due to an organisational downsizing. It was now three years on and he had long since ceased looking for another job. His investments were such that he really had no need to work for an income and now regarded himself as retired from the workplace. During his lifetime, he had seen the horrors of war, had run a business during tough economic times, and was a diligent and intelligent administrator for the firm that eventually retrenched him. Yet, despite having survived so many personal challenges, he was cut to the quick by the circumstances of his forced retirement. Frequently during conversations he would refer to his retrenchment as the time '*they gave me the chop*' and many of those around him suspected that he never really managed to get this hurt out of his system.

As it turns out, the above reaction to forced retirement is very common. Naturally, there are many reasons which drive organisations to restructure with fewer staff. However, those on the receiving end often harbour the feeling that perhaps there was something lacking in their own personal make-up or work performance which caused them to be singled out. These feelings are not helped when those who have been retrenched later see colleagues who they regarded as less talented or less dedicated staying on with the organisation and appearing to prosper.

At a psychological level, involuntary severance from one's livelihood can result in a sense of loss and the need to grieve in much the same way that we do following the loss of a friend or relative. If those who have been retrenched have also closely identified with their job, they may find themselves suffering more than those for whom work was just a means to an end.

Therefore, because of the significant potential for psychological stress due to forced retirement, it was predicted that those people who retired according to their own plans would be better adjusted to retirement than those forced to retire due to:

- illness
- the illness of a family member
- retrenchment, or
- business closure.

What the research found about the effects of forced retirement

As predicted, those retirees who were able to retire voluntarily reported lower levels of stress, anxiety and depression, and higher levels of satisfaction with life in retirement, than those for whom retirement was forced.

These findings were also supported by earlier Australian research in which retirees who had retired voluntarily experienced significantly lower levels of stress, anxiety, depression and bad health than those who were forced to retire. Other studies have also found that retiring according to one's plans increases the likelihood of satisfaction with the experience of retirement.

Given the present trends of restructuring and merging organisations, the above findings are disturbing. The increasing moves to flatter organisational structures, lower staff numbers due to technology, and the outsourcing of business services are resulting in increasing numbers of people being forced to retire against their will. Consequently, those retirees who find themselves forced to retire because of health issues, or due to organisational restructure or closure, need to be aware that they may be at risk from emotional health problems.* They should also be encouraged to seek counselling if these problems subsequently affect their lives.

* *Research into organisational stress has indicated that those senior managers who make the decisions regarding which people are to be retrenched can themselves experience stress and anxiety that may continue for many years. Part of their stress is attributed to their inability to explain to those who were retrenched that the 'hit lists' often had nothing to do with the individual performance of the employee. One former manager on the* Retire 200 *research stated, 'I sometimes wished that I could show some of my retrenched colleagues how much thought and agonising took place before we arrived at our decisions. I am sure it would have helped soften the blow for many of them!'*

Research Finding Two: Being able to retire at fifty-five or younger – *The impact of our age at retirement*

Anecdotal evidence has long suggested that most of us hold strong views concerning our preferred age of retirement. A survey, conducted by the author just before the *Retire 200* research commenced, indicated that most people presently regarded as 'pre-retirees' (that is, aged forty-five to fifty-five), wished to retire as close to age fifty-five as was financially possible. Only a few on the survey indicated that they wanted to work until the traditional retirement age of sixty-five, with most people stating that only dire financial necessity would drive them to work past the age of sixty-five.

Interestingly, many of those preferring to retire at age fifty-five modified their definition of retiring to mean 'retiring from their present job or employer'. This large group of people held the view that retirement would simply signify a change of occupation. They could then embark on activities of their own choice such as voluntary work or part-time work in a low-stress environment, or starting their own small business.

What the research found about the impact of the age at which we retire

Following the results of the preliminary informal survey, it came as no surprise that those people who were able to retire at age fifty-five, or earlier, were associated with lower levels of anxiety than those retiring later. These findings suggest that those people who can retire at age fifty-five should at least consider this option, providing, of course, that other aspects of their lives – such as their financial preparedness – make this a viable option.

Why those who retired early chose to do so

First, many people told stories of their father's generation of retired men who had worked to the age of sixty-five only to die a short time later. These people described themselves as haunted by the memories of their hard-working relatives who had passed away just as it was time for them to relax and do what they liked.

Second, others told stories of their fathers who were so firmly committed to the work ethic, and to their need to perform the role of provider, that when it came time to retire they simply could not relax. It seemed that it was impossible for them to accept that it was now okay to do what they liked with their day. Consequently, for many of them it was more stressful to relax than it had been to work hard, even where their previous occupation had been intrinsically unsatisfying.

Finally, many people found retiring at age fifty-five appealing because it allowed them to embark on chosen activities and personal challenges while they were still young and healthy enough to do so. Many of these people told stories of their parents or relatives who had planned a trip overseas or around Australia at age sixty-five only to have to cancel their plans because of the unexpected ill health or death of one partner.

At a social level, the above results appear to hold a double-edged sword. On one side, those retiring early from full-time work free up jobs and promotions for younger people still in the throes of raising families and paying off mortgages. Moreover, early retirees also have significant contributions to make to society in the form of voluntary work.

On the downside, it is likely that the trend away from lifelong employment will result in people being employed in a variety of short-term contracts and consultancies. With this trend likely to continue, only those who are well organised will commence and maintain forced savings programs, including superannuation and personal investments, required to fund a comfortable retirement. Furthermore, it is becoming increasingly unlikely that the present age pension can continue to be taken for granted by the growing pool of baby boomers, funded as it will be by shrinking numbers of those in full-time employment.

Research Finding Three: Being financially independent – *Comfort versus subsistence*

At an intuitive level, most people would predict that those who can live off their own investments or superannuation are probably going to be more satisfied with life in retirement than those who have to rely on a government pension.

What the research found about financial independence

The research findings indicated that people who were dependent on government pensions for their income experienced significantly higher levels of depression, anxiety and stress, and lower levels of satisfaction with life in retirement, than those who were financially independent. These findings also support those of earlier studies where poor financial status was found to be a predictor of stress and anxiety in retirement.

The impact of dependence on the government age pension

Income from the age pension was regarded by most as barely adequate to provide the basics of life. In most cases, only those who were completely debt free and prepared to live extremely simple lifestyles were able to live on the pension with any success.

CREATIVE ACCOUNTING

Living on the age pension forced people to become very creative when it came to reducing their living costs. Some people had almost turned the process into an art form and had developed a number of strategies for getting by. For example, one woman and her husband collected discarded supermarket receipts that had special offers on the back such as 'two meals for the price of one' at the local hotel. Having had their two-for-one dinner in the main lounge they would go to the gaming section, not to gamble but to finish their meal with the free coffees and after-dinner mints provided for the gambling patrons.

BEING IN DEBT ON THE PENSION

Those who found themselves on the pension while still paying off home mortgages were usually in a precarious financial position. Carrying debt into retirement occurred for any one of a number of reasons.

- Some had experienced a failed second marriage while on the rebound from the death of a lifelong partner. The resulting divorce then required them to refinance their home late in life to buy out their estranged partner's interest in the house.
- A number of people had borrowed against the security of their homes to help adult children in trouble with drugs or personal debts, or who were trying to escape abusive relationships.
- Others had fallen into debt due to failed businesses where the family home had comprised the lender's security.

SOCIAL ACTIVITY

Otherwise simple decisions to participate, or not to participate, in social events were complicated by lack of money. In a number of cases men complained that staying back 'for a couple of beers' after bowls or golf was out of the question. They simply could not afford it. One man described himself feeling like a child again having to ask his partner's permission to spend a few dollars. Others found it embarrassing to have to give excuses for not attending social events because of their lack of disposable income.

ILL HEALTH

For those who became ill or infirm, financial dependency left them feeling frightened and vulnerable to what they felt were the whims of an uncaring health system. Relying on the public health system may not be such an issue when we are young; however, as we become older we may find ourselves suffering from a range of potentially life-threatening complaints such as hypertension, diabetes or heart disease. It is then understandable to feel threatened by the inability to nominate where, when, and with whom required medical procedures or advice are sought.

RUNNING OUT OF MONEY

A number of people described the fortnightly indignity of running out of money one or two days before pension day and being forced to subsist on rice or potatoes until the next pension payment was received. This situation was by no means rare and it is a sobering experience to listen to someone describe how demoralised they feel each time the money runs out. At a psychological level, the situation can be compounded where adult children who could and would provide assistance are blissfully unaware that their proud parent is suffering in silence.

VOLUNTARY WORK

The ability to contribute to society and mix with others through voluntary work was also denied to many people who were struggling to make ends meet on the pension. Voluntary work usually ends up costing the volunteer money in the form of fuel or fares and many could not afford these extra costs.

Research Finding Four: Engaging in 'Purposeful Activities' of more than five hours per week – *The spice of life*

It makes sense that those who keep themselves busy will fare better emotionally than those who lie around doing nothing. Similarly, if an activity has a purpose most people would predict that it would be more rewarding than just remaining active for the sake of 'something to do'.

'Purposeful Activity' was the term used in the *Retire 200* study to describe an activity that had a goal or purpose. For example, playing golf was not regarded as a Purposeful Activity regardless of what most golfers would argue! However, voluntary work in an opportunity shop to raise money for the Brotherhood of Saint Laurence, or working in a paid capacity to supplement retirement income, were examples of Purposeful Activities.

What the research found about the importance of 'Purposeful Activities'

Involvement of over five hours per week in a Purposeful Activity, or a range of Purposeful Activities, was associated with significantly higher satisfaction with life, and with lower levels of depression and stress. Participating in Purposeful Activities was a behaviour that retirees either planned for before retirement, or sought after retirement due to boredom. Therefore, those retirees who found their lives lacking variety or rewarding activities could choose to commence Purposeful Activities virtually at any time during their retirement years.

Eighty-six per cent of those on the *Retire 200* program regarded involvement in a Purposeful Activity as very important to their satisfaction with life. The beneficial effects of involvement in Purposeful Activities continued to show a positive trend even where these activities exceeded thirty hours per week. These findings imply that many of the social and emotional rewards previously provided by the workplace can also be provided by Purposeful Activities in retirement. This notion is supported by the fact that income was cited as the sole motivation for having a Purposeful Activity by only two per cent of participants.

Research Finding Five: Having someone on whom you could rely for emotional support – *Availability of 'a shoulder to cry on'*

'Keep emotionally close to your family – some people forget their family while they are traipsing around the country.'

It was decided to examine the level of emotional support that retirees could access *should they require it.* The basis for investigating availability of emotional support was twofold:

- For many people, the workplace provides a source of informal counselling, where workmates discuss events going on in their lives and provide each other with emotional support during times of crisis. On retirement, these social networks disappear virtually overnight.
- Second, as we get older, the higher the statistical probability becomes that we will suffer from ill health, or that our partner or a friend will become ill or die. When any of these events occurs it is important to have access to people to turn to for extended emotional support.

What the research found about the availability of emotional support

Those with access to emotional support reported significantly lower stress and higher levels of satisfaction with life in retirement. This finding also supports those of earlier research in which availability of emotional support from family or others was associated with lower levels of anxiety and depression. The findings indicate that retirees should maintain their relationships with family and friends where this is possible. Those who find themselves without access to such emotional support are advised to compile a list of alternative resources such as those provided by religious institutions, municipal counselling services, or telephone-based crisis-referral organisations such as Lifeline.

Research Finding Six: Proactively maintaining your health – *Self-promoted health activities*

While it is clear that poor health is an important factor influencing satisfaction in retirement, there had been very little research examining the effect of proactively contributing to one's good health. Consequently, *self-promoted* health activities were examined for their effect on satisfaction with retirement. Health activities were segmented into three subsets, namely, (i) exercise, (ii) diet, and (iii) annual check-ups.

What the research found about self-promoted health activities

First, those who exercised daily were associated with significantly lower levels of stress when compared to those not exercising, or exercising less frequently than daily. The link between exercise and stress reduction is well known and the present findings also indicated that good physical health was associated with lower stress. Apart from the clear emotional benefits of reduced stress, there are also well-established links between high levels of emotional stress and heart attack and stroke. This is an important implication, as many participants reported that their greatest health-related fears concerned heart attack, stroke and the onset of dementia.

Second, those who moderated their diet by either the amount or type of food consumed were found to experience significantly lower levels of depression than those who did not attend to dietary matters. This is consistent with those findings of research into depressive illnesses where it has been found that those who attempt to take even very small steps to control their situation improve faster than those who do not.

Finally, those who regularly attended to all three of the subsets of health maintenance (exercise, diet, annual check-ups) were associated with significantly lower levels of depression than those who attended to only one or two subsets.

Research Finding Seven: Planning for retirement – *Finances and lifestyle*

When it comes to planning behaviour, we generally fall into one of two types of people:

1. Those who are naturally goal- and strategy-oriented and who are therefore more likely to have action plans in place to meet their goals.
2. Those who are naturally unplanned and who prefer to live life as it comes.

What the research found about retirement planning

Those who planned for their retirement were associated with significantly lower levels of self-reported stress, anxiety and depression, and higher levels of satisfaction with life in retirement when compared with those who did not plan. Interestingly, the research findings indicated that it is not just *financial* planning that is relevant: it is also important to make plans for the type of lifestyle you wish to have. For example, many of those on the *Retire 200* program observed that planning for activities well before retirement had made their transition to retirement much less of a jolt. Their rationale was that if you became involved in a number of activities before you retired, there were more common factors linking your 'pre-retirement life' to your life in retirement.

Research Finding Eight: Receiving pre-retirement advice or education – *The benefits of a sneak preview*

People commencing retirement usually do so having very little objective knowledge of what that lifestyle will entail. This is partly due to the fact that there has been very little accurate information on the effects of retirement lifestyles readily available. Consequently, when people commence retirement they often do so with the expectation of a lifestyle that may have very little to do with reality.

Given the lack of available information, people who are seeking information about retirement have had little choice but to turn to friends and relatives who have retired to try to get a snapshot of life in retirement. The problem with this method is that people's values and expectations vary widely. What may be a satisfying retirement lifestyle for one person may turn out to be unsatisfactory for another.

For others, their perception of life in retirement may be based on a rosy existence that is predicated more on escaping from the workforce than it is on looking forward to an exciting new phase in life. It was therefore decided to examine what effect receiving formal pre-retirement advice or training would have on perceptions and subsequent emotional wellbeing.

What the research found about the effects of receiving pre-retirement advice or education

The research findings indicated that those who sought pre-retirement advice, or who attended pre-retirement training programs, reported significantly lower levels of depression than those who received no pre-retirement advice or training.

These findings support those of earlier research where:

1. There were significant relationships between attendance at a pre-retirement seminar and subsequent wellbeing in retirement.
2. The amount of exposure to pre-retirement advice was positively correlated with retirement satisfaction, and
3. Receiving pre-retirement education was associated with significantly more positive attitudes to life.

SECTION ONE

Personal fulfilment and growth in retirement

'The minute you stop moving forwards you start going backwards.'

The need for continual growth and improvement is well established in business, in scientific research, in sport, and many other areas. There is now no doubt that the same rule applies to our need for personal growth through having a challenging lifestyle when we retire.

Before each participant of the *Retire 200* was accepted into the program, it was necessary to explain to them how the research would work; what their involvement would be; and to answer any questions they had about the process. During these preliminary conversations it became apparent that the people with the most positive attitudes to life seemed to be those who were most heavily involved in an active retirement. This perception was later confirmed during the psychological assessment of each research participant.

At the top end of the scale of retirement satisfaction were those people who regarded retirement as an adventure and who were involved in regular activities that were either creative, or which involved the production of goods or services. Conversely, participants who were depressed or anxious tended to be those for whom retirement was an inactive experience and who had few or no interests or hobbies beyond the daily routine of home maintenance.

The need for a 'Purposeful Activity' became one of the central findings of the study when it came to predicting satisfaction with life in retirement. Chapter One focuses on this important topic.

CHAPTER ONE

Remaining challenged and involved through Purposeful Activities

AIMS OF THIS CHAPTER

- To examine the research findings on the benefits of Purposeful Activities.
- To understand the relevance of Purposeful Activities to satisfaction in retirement.
- To consider your own situation and to determine whether you believe you could benefit from pursuing Purposeful Activities.
- To provide a resource list of potential activities and contacts to pursue.

The topic of staying active was of keen interest to most of the participants on the *Retire 200* program and many had strong opinions that they were keen to see reported in the research. Consequently, in this chapter there will be numerous quotations from research participants concerning their personal motivation for staying active.

The 'honeymoon' period

'Think carefully about the timing of your retirement – you feel euphoric at first but you need to have something to do.'

Those of you who have retired comparatively recently may be saying, 'But I've been retired for three months now – playing golf or fishing four times a week is all I'll ever need to do to keep *me* happy!' The sociologist R. C. Atchley first investigated the retirement honeymoon phase back in the 1960s. His research found that the honeymoon phase typically lasted anywhere from a couple of months to one year from the start of retirement. Closely linked to the honeymoon phase is the common tendency of people to find that their attitudes to life fluctuate from positive to negative for up to five years from commencing retirement.

Typical retirement honeymoon behaviours

It is during the honeymoon period that leisure activities may well be all that we require to remain satisfied. This is probably because it takes most of us about twelve months to work through the range of activities we were looking forward to doing '*when I retire*'. Consequently, people who have loved golf all their lives may find that eighteen holes of golf five days a week is fine for a year or so. Eventually, though, even the keenest golfer can tire of unfettered access to their sport.

Here are some other retirement 'honeymoon' behaviours that were identified during the research program:

- Deciding to do little but read all the books 'I have always wanted to read'.
- Looking for a new house.
- Moving to a new state.
- Going on the planned trip overseas or around Australia.
- Buying a new car.
- Renovating or painting the house.
- Setting up a hobby room or workshop.

Of course, many of these activities really do need to be completed. Many people do choose to renovate their home soon after retiring and such activities can be both practical and realistic. However, the fact remains that where such projects are commenced immediately after full-time work has ceased, the realities of life are, in a sense, put on hold. Newly retired people find themselves pleasantly distracted and kept occupied as they plan for and complete their project. It may not be until after these projects are completed that it dawns on them that their retirement years have now started! This realisation signals the end of the honeymoon period and it is then quite common for people to enter periods of depression, anxiety or stress. This can be a puzzling and frightening experience for those who were anticipating a carefree existence.

'If you have been dedicated to your work you may flounder for the first year.'

There is considerable evidence to suggest that the intensity and duration of the honeymoon phase is linked to the level of satisfaction experienced in immediate pre-retirement work life. If you found your work boring or you were unhappy in your occupation, retirement is more likely to be founded on the need to 'escape' from work rather than on the transition to life in retirement. This can make the onset of emotional problems such as depression doubly perplexing for those who had looked forward to life in retirement for many years.

The impact of Purposeful Activities on retirees' emotional wellbeing

The links between low levels of depression in people who are purposefully active is supported by existing psychological research into clinical depression. People sometimes describe how they were depressed while inactive during their early retirement phase but that this depression lifted once they commenced Purposeful Activities. Similarly, others found that they became depressed after a club or organisation that had been the focus of their Purposeful Activity closed for some reason. When they resumed their activities through another source, the depression lifted.

What are Purposeful Activities?

It became clear from the research with the *Retire 200* that there were three levels of activity undertaken by people.

- No activities: apart from the daily routine of eating, sleeping, shopping, watching TV, reading.
- Leisure activities: such as gardening, fishing, golf.
- Purposeful Activities: where something is produced or achieved, or where a service is provided.

Many people cited gardening as their Purposeful Activity. For example:

- For some people the principal motivation for gardening activities was not just related to essential maintenance but to reduce grocery costs through growing their own produce.
- Some people regarded gardening as a highly pleasurable pastime that provided the types of release from stress found in meditation and other hobbies.
- Others were motivated by the prospect of entering gardening competitions, developing new strains of roses or growing the largest pumpkin.

One woman established a very large garden that she dedicated to the memory of her husband, and which was open to the public.

In each of these cases gardening was regarded as a Purposeful Activity because it was clearly linked to a secondary goal. However, just mowing the lawn or weeding the garden to stop it 'taking over the house' was not regarded as a Purposeful Activity but, rather, a maintenance exercise such as cleaning or painting the house.

Other examples of Purposeful Activities are: paid or voluntary work, craft or artistic hobbies, renovating a house, undertaking study or short courses, active membership of service organisations, or active membership of clubs such as PROBUS.

For how many hours a week do I need to be purposely active?

Those people on the *Retire 200* program who spent five hours or more per week involved in Purposeful Activities were:

- less depressed
- less anxious
- less stressed
- more satisfied with their general experience of life in retirement.

As the *Retire 200* study progressed, a wide variation in the time spent in activities emerged. Some people had no structured activity to occupy their time and tended just to potter around. Others were active for many hours per week – in one case, a Tasmanian retiree was involved in activities that totalled a staggering eighty hours per week! The average number of hours per week spent in a Purposeful Activity was 23 hours for males and 17.3 hours for females. Interestingly, the closer the hours per week approached those previously spent at work, so did the trend move towards lower stress, lower anxiety, lower depression, and higher satisfaction with life in retirement.

The above results are very important. They indicate that **having a Purposeful Activity in retirement is not just some form of minor distraction – it is a significant component of a well-balanced, happy retirement!**

What motivates people to become involved in Purposeful Activities?

When the information supplied by the participants of the *Retire 200* research was examined, it became clear that there were fifteen distinct reasons that motivated people to become active in retirement.

The fifteen motivators

1. The desire for status.
2. The desire for creativity and production.
3. The desire for an interest.
4. The desire for having goals.
5. The desire to plan.
6. The desire to 'run the business I've always wanted'.
7. The desire to replace work.
8. The desire for balance.

9. The desire for structure.
10. The desire to be busy.
11. The desire for fun.
12. The desire for mental and physical stimulation.
13. The desire to mix with people and create social networks.
14. The desire for adventure.
15. The desire to produce income.

Not surprisingly, most of these motivators have also been found to impact positively on job satisfaction in the workplace. In other words, having Purposeful Activities in retirement can provide many of the same rewards that involvement in a satisfying work environment gave us when we were engaged in full-time work.

We will now examine these motivators in more detail.

Reason one: *To fulfil the desire for status*

Status is often found near the top of the list of motivators of job satisfaction. Consequently, organisations around the world endeavour to create status symbols that will help them produce the best work environment for retaining and motivating their employees.

The desire for status can be very high for some individuals. For those who have retired, the loss of their previous occupation may also mean the loss of status. In some cases, the status symbol may not be a benefit such as a company-provided car but, rather, the status of full-time employment and all it represents in society.

'If you have been in a profession you have status – when you retire you need to hang on to being a person "of value".'

This comment came from a research participant who was a retired doctor – he had built up a substantial practice while also holding the position of chairman of the board of a large private hospital.

Soon after he retired, he and his wife sold their inner-city home and moved to a property in the country. Their income from investments was substantial and their health was excellent, but they were now both 'unknown' in their new town. The former greetings and constant recognition in the street which had once bordered on the intrusive were now missed and the doctor soon found that he was experiencing moderate depression.

Some months after the *Retire 200* research program concluded, the doctor rang to say that he had commenced working as a locum for a couple of days a week and that his wife was now involved in charity work. Community involvement and its attendant status had returned to their lives and they were happy again.

Similarly, people involved in Purposeful Activities can find that important and visible roles such as being the club treasurer, or arranging scheduling for the delivery of meals on wheels, can offer the status formerly provided by their full-time occupation.

Reason two: *To fulfil the desire for creativity and production*

'Have a hobby where you actually produce something – not just golf. I have seen friends retire without an activity and they die!'

'Get a hobby – preferably a creative one – not just knocking a golf ball around – you need to see something for your work.'

As we have already seen, the dream of some people to spend their retirement playing golf, or to go fishing, often sours once the novelty wears off. It was also clear during the research that having a Purposeful Activity with a creative component was very important to some people. The sense of achievement that they gained from doing something creative represented the driving force behind their commitment to activities. Consequently, the range of items produced by participants on the *Retire 200* program was staggering. Some participants who had an interest in woodwork or metalwork built furniture and other items which they either used themselves or gave to family and friends. Others donated their products to charities, or sold them at markets or to specialist retailers. One man with an engineering background and a large workshop produced a flywheel for use in a community project to restore an old steam engine.

Reason three: *To fulfil the desire for an interest*

'You need to seek out an interest or activity, for example, investing on the stock exchange.'

'Retirement gives the freedom to choose activities but you need to have a notion of how you are going to spend your time – what activities you will choose.'

The two quotations above highlight an interesting difference in the way that people viewed their newfound freedom from full-time employment. Some regarded free time as something that they desperately needed to fill with activity and were concerned that they might have difficulty finding enough to do. Others approached retirement with the view that there were many options available – you simply needed to select the best activities from the range available. Such people would express their exasperation at some of their peers who complained that they were bored, noting that in their own case they had trouble finding enough time to do all the things they wanted to during the week!

Reason four: *To fulfil the desire for having goals*

'You need to be a professional manager in retirement. Regard yourself as a small business with goals, a mission statement.'

'The flexibility of retirement can bring on a *mañana* mindset – you still need to plan, that is, to have goals to achieve.'

'Have a reason to get up each morning – have a goal for that day, especially one involving social contact.'

'Have more goals in retirement than when you were at work – join groups such as PROBUS.'

'Project your activities and plans well into the future – have a goal or an outing to look forward to.'

Later in the book we will look at the impact of our personality, and that of others, on our life in retirement. Regardless of what personality preferences we have, most of us enjoy having an activity to which we can look forward. It was this aspect of planning that many people felt was critical to their enjoyment of life. Consequently, a number of people used a wall calendar on which they recorded future events such as PROBUS meetings, lunch with a friend, visiting the grandchildren, or a trip interstate. Being able to see a range of activities and interests stretching out into the future was their psychological buffer against feelings of aimlessness.

Reason five: *To fulfil the desire to plan*

'Plan well in advance what you are going to do – think about what interests you want to continue or develop.'

'Prepare for retirement – make sure you have a lot of interests – don't put your feet up – don't move into idleness – make sure that you have enough money to support your interests.'

'Plan things – travel.'

Closely linked to the need to have goals is the need to plan. Essentially, the difference between the two is that having a goal represents the 'destination', while planning involves designing the logistics of 'how you are going to get there'.

Planning continues to be important throughout retirement. It includes planning finances so that there is money available for a holiday, planning where you will go on your holiday, and planning what you will do while you are away.

Planning also removes the great fear of many that inertia will overtake them. By having clearly stated goals, they felt they were less likely to fritter away their time through idleness.

Reason six: *To fulfil the desire to 'run the business I've always wanted'*

Several people, particularly those who had spent a lifetime employed by someone else, were keen to try running a small business. While the desire to bring in additional retirement income was a significant motivator in some of these cases, there were also other reasons which were just as important.

- First, there was the desire of some people to prove to themselves that they had 'what it takes' to build a small business into a successful profit-making venture. In many cases, the pleasure gained from achieving even small successes far outweighed the benefits gained from the income itself.
- Second, there was the keen sense of involvement gained from planning, and then executing the plan, as they ran their new business.
- Finally, there was the social contact that was intrinsic to the running of many businesses as the business owners interacted with customers and suppliers.

One man started by purchasing items of clothing that were 'seconds', which he sold from his car boot at markets. As he made a profit, he was able to gradually purchase more stock and eventually diversified into selling 'nibbles' such as peanuts and potato chips. During the research interview he was anxious to establish that, while income had been his initial motivator, the social interaction with customers and other stall-holders was now one of the most important contributing factors to his wellbeing.

Note: As many new business ventures fail, think carefully before you commit hard-earned retirement savings to a business venture.

Reason seven: ***To fulfil the desire to replace work***

'The more you have been vocationally involved, the harder it is to adjust to retirement.'

'I missed the challenges of work very much in the first twelve months.'

'Have a routine to differentiate weekends from weekdays otherwise everything becomes grey.'

'Professionals want to exercise their minds – I was used to high stress – I miss stress and feel like a prisoner.'

'Keep alive intellectually – understand the wider issues impacting on society otherwise you relinquish your professionalism.'

'Have things in place to replace your job.'

'I found that it is hard to handle the psychology of leaving a high-stress job to doing nothing.'

'Business people/teachers etc need hobbies/interests.'

As you would imagine, there have been countless studies on what it is that motivates us to like or dislike work. The motivating factors for work are segmented into two broad categories: *intrinsic* motivation that relates to the work itself, and *extrinsic* motivation, which refers to rewards that are external to the work. As you examine the following list of intrinsic and extrinsic motivators in the workplace, you will see that most of them also apply to the benefits of having Purposeful Activities.

INTRINSIC MOTIVATORS:

- The satisfaction gained from using a skill for which you are trained.
- The satisfaction gained from doing a job well.
- The satisfaction gained from the challenges presented by the task.
- The satisfaction gained from confirming to yourself that you are a skilled or valuable person.

EXTRINSIC MOTIVATORS:

- Promotion and status.
- Money – pay or bonuses.
- Recognition – for example, being recognised by your peers as hard working, or as skilled in a particular area.
- Benefits/perks – for example, the use of the president's car space at your club.
- Access to social networks, work friends.

Reason eight: ***To fulfil the desire for balance***

'Balance your interests with seeing people.'

'It is vital to have a wide range of interests otherwise I get depressed.'

'Have something to do and also have periods to do nothing.'

The need for having balance in our lives is a recurring theme probably best summed up by the old expression 'The grass is always greener on the other side of the fence.' When we are at work, many of us long to be on holidays. As a long holiday draws to a close some people will say, *'I'm looking forward to getting back to work – I feel recharged now.'*

The notion of balance is a recurring theme in the physical sciences, in politics, in philosophy, and in psychology. Balance is also at the heart of the concept of 'everything in moderation', which those in the various health sciences typically espouse. Here are some examples of how the concept of balance occurs across a range of life situations.

1. HOMEOSTASIS

The tendency of our body to try to re-establish equilibrium when various components get out of balance, for example, salt levels, sugar levels, or white and red cell levels. At a psychological level, homeostasis also explains why we eventually need a break when we are overworked, or require challenges when we have been inactive for too long.

2. MIND VERSUS BODY

Does the way we think influence the way we feel, or does the way we feel influence the way we think? Medical and psychological research indicates that there is a strong relationship between the two. We therefore need to ensure that we remain well in both areas for true health.

3. NATURE VERSUS NURTURE

What influences our behaviour more, our genetic make-up, or the environment in which we are raised? The debate continues to rage despite increasingly sophisticated methods of examining genetic effects, and in spite of the many studies of twins separated at birth and brought up in different environments. The answer to this question is that it is probably a balance of the two influences.

4. FACILITATING ANXIETY VERSUS STRESS

Most people will have heard of the term 'good stress'. It refers to the need we all have to be challenged enough to stimulate interest – in psychology this stimulation is referred to as 'facilitating anxiety'. However, if anxiety levels become too high due to increased workloads, or to unreasonable degrees of difficulty, then we suffer from stress and become *dis*tressed. Alternatively, if we are understimulated we become bored and anxious. The key is a healthy balance between being challenged and participating in sufficient recreation.

5. YIN VERSUS YANG

The terms *yin* and *yang* refer to the Chinese philosophy that describes the universe as comprising two opposing forces. The philosophy states that the yin, which represents the passive aspects of life, needs to be balanced with the yang, which represents the active aspects of life.

Reason nine: ***To fulfil the desire for structure***

'Keep a full diary to look forward to things.'

'Gear up with an initial weekly schedule.'

'Learn to live without the structure of work – take steps to keep busy.'

'Have some structure in your life.'

'Need to have things you *have* to do to keep motivated.'

'Aim to find happiness in "daily" events rather than striving for success.'

'Have a "subject" to address each day.'

For some of us, the structure provided by the workplace was a curse that restricted our freedom; for others, it provided a sense of security. Whatever we felt about work, the mad rush at breakfast time to catch the 7.04 train, or to arrive at work in time for the 8 a.m. sales meeting, provided us with structured activities from Monday to Friday. If we did not conform, we lost our jobs.

Some occupations are associated with very high levels of structure. For those retiring from the military, leaving that highly structured environment can be quite unnerving. One man on the *Retire 200* program had been a highly ranked officer in one of the armed forces. Soon after retiring, he was involved in a car accident that he attributed to his lack of driving experience after years of having a car and driver as part of his position. For other retired military personnel, the 'Friday afternoon – Monday morning' suddenness of the transition from a highly structured environment to an unstructured environment was very stressful, leading in some cases to significant levels of anxiety and depression.

Like their military counterparts, men and women working in blue-collar occupations such a factory-assembly lines were often accustomed to working in a supervised work environment. This environment, while restrictive at one level, provided clear behavioural boundaries and a sense of security. One former blue-collar worker, from a large industrial organisation, recognised the importance of structure to his own sense of wellbeing and, on retiring, imposed his own!

'I have set up a tool-making workshop in our double garage next to the house. Each weekday I get up at the same time that I did when I was working, change into my overalls, and have breakfast. Straight after breakfast, I go to the workshop and work until lunchtime. I take an hour off for lunch that I have with my wife back in the house. After lunch I return to the workshop until I knock off at four.'

Not too many people would wish to impose this level of discipline on themselves! Nevertheless, apart from providing structure, the discipline this man applied to himself allowed him to continue to enjoy utilising his skills as a qualified toolmaker while making parts of cars for his friends in a vintage car club, thereby saving them costly repairs.

Reason ten: ***To fulfil the desire to be busy***

'Have plenty to do.'

'Don't sit and watch the traffic go by.'

'Take up something that you really like and get stuck into it – go flat out to keep busy.'

'Don't vegetate – keep busy.'

'Be fully occupied – put in a full day doing the things that you enjoy – mix with people you can help and whose company you can enjoy.'

'It's a case of "drones" versus "actives" – drones die of boredom.'

We all enjoy having challenges and to be able to function as normal, intelligent human beings. Lying in a hammock on a tropical island may look ideal on a travel brochure but, as most of us eventually realise, it is not active or challenging enough to keep us satisfied in the long term. As the people quoted above suggest, we need to be busy and our first job after retiring should be to seek out clubs, activities and other interests that will keep us occupied.

Reason eleven: *To fulfil the desire for fun*

'Don't feel immobilised about sticking to your original plan – being able to move on is important – have fun – use lateral thinking – please yourself.'

'Stay interested and active – PROBUS is good.'

'Try different voluntary roles until you find one that makes you happy.'

'Do what you "want" to do, not what you "have" to do.'

'I started out by joining everything – but you eventually decide to cut out all but those activities that are enjoyable.'

'To each his own regarding activities – you must choose a club or activity that suits *you* and keeps you busy.'

'Do the fun things you haven't had time for in your working life.'

'Work with a group where you like the people – if you find that they get on your goat, get out.'

Fun, like beauty, is very much in the eye of the beholder. The people on the *Retire 200* research provided two recurring pieces of advice when it came to ensuring that they built fun into their lives. First, many commented that after a life working hard to pay the bills, discharge the mortgage and educate the kids, it was now *their* time to lighten up and have some fun. One man, who spent much of his time visiting the terminally ill, also recognised the need to have activities that were light-hearted and pleasurable. In his particular case the fun gained from taking a day trip to the country gave him the opportunity to recharge his batteries so that he could continue to offer a quality service when visiting the hospital.

The second point relating to fun came from those people who had been so determined to remain active that they were now overcommitted, or were involved in activities that they were not enjoying. One woman had started out recording books for the blind soon after retiring. Without really intending to, she soon found herself recording three days per week. In the end, it was simply too much time out of her schedule and she eventually reduced the load to free herself up for other activities.

Reason twelve: *To fulfil the desire for mental and physical stimulation*

'Be busy mentally and physically.'

'Choose activities that are useful and that involve mental and physical work.'

'I need a hobby – something to think about.'

'Plan to have something to do to keep active at three levels: (i) physical, (ii) mental, and (iii) spiritual; at the spiritual level it can either be religion or your personal code, your way of life – it doesn't matter.'

'Do something to keep mentally and physically active – organise activity (even if it requires training).'

'You need to prepare alternative activities that involve mental/physical stimulation and social contact, for example, PROBUS.'

The people quoted here all had one goal in common: they did not wish to atrophy, and many of them were fond of using the expression '*use it or lose it*'. We need to keep our minds and bodies functioning and vital by using them. You only have to think back to a time when you have been bedridden, even for just a few days, to gain insight into the comparative weakness that you experience from not using your muscles. After longer illnesses we may find that it also takes a while to get our minds back into gear. This situation is no different in retirement if we move from the challenges of full-time work to an inactive lifestyle.

Reason thirteen: *To fulfil the desire to mix with people and create social networks*

'Join a club – mix with people.'

'Plan to have what you need to have around you (social networks).'

'Ensure you have something to enjoy – an interest where you meet people.'

'Keep yourself occupied – mentally and physically – keep mixing with people.'

For most people, Purposeful Activity involves contact with others. Depending on our individual need to socialise, contact may range from regular interaction in the form of membership of committees or through other activities involving contact with others. For some, social contact may just involve spasmodic contact with friends and neighbours. However, it is important for all of us to ensure that we have some contact with others at least weekly where possible – social isolation is not good for us, as we will discuss later in this book.

Reason fourteen: *To fulfil the desire for adventure*

'Leave yourself open to "unlikely suggestions", for example, running community activities.'

'Be prepared to change – be happy – do things that make you happy – look at all the options.'

Only a few people cited the need for adventure as a desirable part of their retirement experience. One particularly adventurous participant of the *Retire 200* program decided halfway to an Asian destination to get off the plane at the next airport and to stay in that country for six months, just to 'see what it was like'. While he reportedly had a wonderful time, this type of spontaneous behaviour is certainly not for everyone.

Other people used retirement to realise lifelong dreams. One man in his sixties spent two years learning to fly a light aircraft. Once he felt he had achieved his ambition, he ceased flying, now satisfied that he had achieved his goal and had survived at the same time! Less than five kilometres from this man's home in Adelaide, a woman in her late sixties had decided that she was going to try parachuting at least once in her life. At the time we spoke she had made five jumps and was eagerly looking forward to her next.

The above examples represented some of the more dramatic activities undertaken by people to meet their needs for adventure. However, what comprises adventure for one person is not necessarily adventurous to another. The need for adventure was also a driving motivation for all those people who embarked on trips around Australia, went on an overseas trip, or started a business.

Reason fifteen: *To fulfil the desire/need to produce income*

Those people who worked to produce income tended to fall into one of two categories.

First, there were those who cheerfully welcomed work because of the opportunities for activity and social interaction. For them, income was an important but secondary goal. In several of these instances, the part-time job involved helping out in the business of an adult child, or returning to work part-time in the business they had established some years before. For others, it was consulting or working part-time for a local business. Many of these people commented that they regularly had to decline offers of longer hours from employers delighted to find an enthusiastic and reliable worker.

Second, there were those people who were forced to work and who found this situation irksome. Some of these people were victims of unexpected marriage break-ups in later life. In such instances, women were particularly badly affected, as often their superannuation was inadequate due to their comparatively short time in the workforce, or due to their level of pay. Other people had to work due to the loss of a business or farm. In some cases, the business failure had also included the loss of their family home as part of the business loan guarantee.

Ways to use Purposeful Activities to enrich your life

Planning for activities before you retire

'Have creative interests years prior to retirement so that you don't notice the jolt. If you leave it until you retire you will be disappointed in your lack of skills.'

'Before you retire, start building bridges so that you have something to do in retirement.'

'Get involved in things you like before you retire because retirement is a shock to the system and you can lose the self-confidence to start something new – you should have a lot of things you like doing.'

'Think realistically about what to do *before* you retire – have a lot of things to do.'

'You should develop interests before retirement and move smoothly into them at retirement.'

'When you are still working, develop interests apart from work – then put them into action.'

'Get involved in clubs, U3A, charity – start exploring options – subscribe to relevant publications.'

'Think about all the things you want to do – plan – don't walk into an empty space – do it well in advance of leaving work.'

In some parts of the world, it is common for larger organisations and government departments to offer employees the opportunity to phase down from full employment gradually so that they are not thrown into retirement overnight. Research into this concept has confirmed the benefits of allowing people to wind down progressively for a couple of years before retirement. Such schemes typically work by introducing a four-day week for some months, then a three-day week for a further few months and so on. At the same time people in the pre-retirement phase of work receive counselling on how best to prepare for their new lifestyle.

Unfortunately, pre-retirement schemes of the type described above are not entrenched in Australian corporate or government work cultures. Nevertheless, a number of participants had individually approached their employers and arranged to work for four- or three-day weeks for the last year of their time with the organisation.* Others took it upon themselves to insure against a 'jolt' at retirement by commencing a number of activities well before the date. By creating continuity of activities spanning pre-retirement and retirement life, these people were able to 'smooth' the transition.

* *If you are still working and are thinking of this option, be sure to first check the possible negative impacts such a move will have on your superannuation retirement benefit. In some superannuation*

plans, a reduction in income during the last year(s) of work may reduce the amount paid on retirement.

The unsuspecting computer expert

'Patricia' lives in a large regional city. Soon after she retired, she was approached by one of her friends who wanted to learn the basics of a computer word-processing package. Her friend was compiling a family history and had found that typing and retyping pages of information was holding her back from producing a quality product.

As Patricia pondered the best way to teach a beginner the computer skills she had acquired over a number of years, an idea dawned. Surely, if her friend wanted to learn about computers there would be others in a similar position. Moreover, word-processing was only one computer skill that she had picked up . . . she was also skilled at using electronic spreadsheets and presentation packages.

Having first used her friend as a guinea pig, Patricia placed a small advertisement in the local paper. In her advertisement, Patricia explained that her courses were low cost, easy for beginners to follow, and were fun to do.

Gradually the business built up as satisfied customers told their friends. Patricia was now in business and had a paying Purposeful Activity.

Have a range of activities in case of health problems

'Have options in case you lose physical ability.'

Your state of health clearly affects the type of activities in which you can participate. One woman described her intense frustration when the onset of rheumatoid arthritis forced her to give up painting quite early in retirement. She had previously envisaged a lifestyle in which she would fulfil her dream to paint full time and augment her income by selling paintings at craft markets.

A few people were so concerned about the prospect of ill health that they developed a range of activities in case a particular body function failed due to arthritis, heart attack or stroke. Consequently, their activities included such diverse pursuits as golf, walking, computing, reading, and memberships or management of clubs or other organisations. If a prolonged period of illness then precluded one or more of the activities, there were still others that could be accessed.

Be 'active' in your activities

'You have got to become active and involved and not just in one thing.'

'Don't just go along to clubs and have others organise everything for you – the ones who do the organising are the ones who get the most out of it and enjoy it the most.'

'Enjoy every day.'

A realistic view of activities – borne of experience

No doubt, you have heard of the job experience programs where teenagers in the final years of their secondary schooling spend some time working in an occupational setting such as an office or department store. One of the most significant learning outcomes from work experience comes from the opportunity to compare the realities of day-to-day work life with one's perceptions of the role.

For some students, work experience confirms that they are on the right track and should continue their plans to undertake study to qualify as an architect or as a teacher. For others, the experience is a rude awakening when they may learn that life as a corporate lawyer is nothing like that portrayed in their favourite TV show.

Unfortunately, in Australia few 'retirement experience' programs are available to allow us to experience life in retirement before the actual event! However, issues concerning unrealistic perceptions of retirement are just as common as those of young people seeking information regarding a career.

'I used to love playing in the jazz band one night a week at the pub, and dreamed of the day when I could play on all the day gigs too. I soon learned that day-work for a full-time jazz musician involves engagements such as playing in ghastly shopping centres. Here members of the band may find themselves traipsing up and down escalators following luminaries like Father Christmas or the Easter Bunny to promote a store sale.'

'I was going to sit in the sun and read books but I haven't had time.'

The above comments confirm that our perceptions of retirement are not always congruent with reality. People regularly mentioned that the laidback lifestyle they had expected turned out to be busy and fulfilling, with spare time being as scarce as when they were working.

Motivation – it takes effort to start

'You may have to force yourself to be active – but then it is rewarding.'

'One shouldn't wait for things to happen – get involved in things, for example, consultancies, activities for the mind, get involved in the community.'

'Don't sit around and be lonely – become involved.'

'You need to have interesting things to do – but you still need incentive.'

'A lot of retirees go into their shell and don't want to participate.'

'Keep motivated – keep interested (turn off the TV) – keep learning.'

'Don't give up – look for something you like to do.'

'Don't sit on your backside – go out and make it happen.'

'You've got to be ready and mentally prepared to have activities – if you can also earn from them, fine!'

'Look at what your friends do and get ideas – keep busy otherwise you dwell on problems.'

Some people are naturally well organised and put their ideas into action quickly after conceiving them. Similarly, there are those who are so extraverted that their high need for contact with people automatically drives them to seek social activities on a regular basis. For many of us, however, it takes real effort to join new clubs or organisations, or to push ourselves to investigate potential activities. Where people are having trouble getting started in new activities, particularly where it involves joining in with groups of people, it may be due to one or more of the following reasons:

1. *You are not sure what is expected of you and may feel nervous about starting at the new club or activity.*
   Suggestion: Do some research. Find out what people wear there, what is expected of members and how formal or informal the meetings are. This will help you relax when you realise that you will fit in after all.

2. *You feel you will be inadequate and will be rejected by others.* **Suggestion**: Do more research. Try to find out whether the activity is one you see yourself enjoying. Will the people there be good company for you? Are they the type of people you like mixing with?

3. *You are concerned that the benefits to be gained from participating may be outweighed by the personal efforts/costs required.* **Suggestion**: Ask yourself if this is just an excuse to put off making an effort. 'Am I just trying to take the easy way out here?'

The impact of aging on Purposeful Activities

'People need to think of the impact of aging on their lifestyle in retirement – I started an orchard but didn't think through how much physical hard work would be involved. You need, therefore, to get advice on what to expect – not just today but down the track when you are older.'

Only a few of the people on the *Retire 200* program raised the issue of the impact of aging on their decision to establish a Purposeful Activity. Yet the relevance of aging is significant, particularly where capital is invested in an income-producing activity such as the farm described above. The man concerned had purchased a property with the intention of setting up a fruit orchard. He had done all the right things such as conducting market research, learning to run a profitable farm, and he had identified the specific agricultural issues pertinent to growing fruit. He was soon running a successful business. His problem, however, arose from the fact that much of the hard work of harvesting and pruning came years later, when the orchard was established. By then he was older and was beginning to suffer from arthritis, which hampered his ability to perform some tasks around the farm. Had he known the level of hard physical work required, and the fact that he was going to develop arthritis, he probably would still have pursued his dream. However, more informed planning would have enabled him to prepare better for the time when he would need to delegate some work around the farm to others.

Avoid destructive activities

'Don't get involved in destructive activities, for example, playing the poker machines.'

The destructive financial effects of poker machines horrified this woman. She spoke of people she knew who had lost most of their life savings and, in one case, their home. She believed that many of these people were simply lonely and that the enticing environment of the gaming rooms conspired to give them a misguided sense of purpose and belonging.

Excessive alcohol consumption was also a problem for some people, particularly those who lived alone. Again, while some would have certainly been suffering from alcoholism before retirement, many heavy drinkers claimed they overindulged due to the boredom brought on by a lack of meaningful activities.

Sources of Purposeful Activities

The range of potential Purposeful Activities is limited only by your imagination. Here are a few ideas to help you get the ball rolling.

Speak with other people who have retired

Ask others what they do with their time in retirement. Keep asking – don't just stop after you have spoken to one or two people. Eventually you will find someone who has a Purposeful Activity that appeals to you.

Form a Purposeful Activities task force

If you have friends for whom finding a suitable activity is also an issue, set up a Purposeful Activities task force. Hold regular meetings over a cup of coffee and generate ideas together for things to do. During the meeting, set everyone the task of seeking out five people with whom they will discuss the search for Purposeful Activities. Then reconvene the meeting in a fortnight and have everyone report on their findings. Warn everyone in advance to be positive and to persist so that no one has any excuses for coming back without some ideas.

PROBUS

PROBUS is an acronym for Professional and Business. It is an organisation for retired people from such occupational backgrounds – however, in most cases this requirement is not enforced. PROBUS clubs vary in their levels of activity, with some clubs inviting both sexes and others for either men or women. Some clubs arrange outings for their members and may have regular meetings with a guest speaker.

Your local library

Visit your local library and check the noticeboard for any clubs or activities that may be listed there. You can also check the library's website for more information. Ask the librarian for any local contacts or ideas they may have.

Your municipal office

Most municipalities produce a booklet once a year that lists the activities and clubs in their area. Here you will find contact telephone numbers for your local PROBUS clubs. Also check the websites of your neighbouring municipalities – they too may have contacts that are close enough to be accessed by you. The other reason for looking wider than your own municipality is that some are better than others – if your own municipality is a little impoverished for contacts, the others nearby may be better.

Your local papers

Notices and articles about coming events are often reported in the local newspaper. For example, you may discover an article about a club or association that you find interesting. These papers are also a good way of keeping in touch with issues affecting your immediate community.

U3A

This acronym stands for University of the Third Age. It is designed to meet the needs of people in retirement who wish to explore an area of interest but who do not want to sit for exams or pay high fees. U3A is run on a local basis and your library or municipal office will have the details of the nearest campus. Both the participants and the lecturers are predominantly retirees. The lecturing staff provide their time on a voluntary basis and may be former university lecturers or people with a particular skill.

Short courses

In each state, institutions provide short courses for adults for a reasonable fee. In Victoria, for example, the Council of Adult Education runs such courses – if you are in another state your local library or a search on the Internet may be able to provide you with the right contact.

Voluntary work

Many organisations will be grateful for your help. If you wish to donate your services, try the local charities, churches, or hospitals as a starting point. The type of help you can provide can be direct to those in need – such as delivering meals on wheels – or indirect, such as helping on fundraising committees of service organisations like Lions, Rotary, or the women's group Zonta.

Form an interest group

Some people start their own interest groups. Such groups do not have to be large or difficult to arrange. For example, if you are interested in the Internet, you could find a couple of friends with similar interests and meet once a month to discuss the latest websites. Those friends could then invite other friends and the group would grow, as you desired.

A case study: Fay and Ron

When it comes to ensuring that they are involved in Purposeful Activities, Fay and Ron set a cracking pace. Their range of activities is as diverse as their commitment is substantial.

Fay is a retired bookkeeper – her activities include the following:

Secretary of the local PROBUS club where she also attends to the mailing and agendas for club meetings.	2 hours per week
Committee member for a local nursing home where she also helps organise their fundraising fetes.	2 hours per week
Visits her mother each evening in the nursing home to feed her and provide company. On the weekends she also visits at lunchtimes.	8 hours per week
Running her own beauty therapy business.	20 hours per week

Works as an experienced dressmaker. Sometimes this involves a small amount of time per week. On other occasions, Fay has been known to work into the small hours of the morning to finish off a wedding gown and bridesmaids' dresses.	Varies
Secretary of the local jazz club, attending to the minutes, agendas, correspondence, and a food platter for the band at the monthly club functions.	2 hours per week

In addition to the above activities, Fay maintains the home for herself, her husband, Ron, and their adult daughter. Fay tries to take Tuesdays off – but, not surprisingly, she does not always succeed in meeting this goal!

Ron is a retired corporate secretary and qualified accountant – his activities include the following:

Newsletter editor for the local jazz club. Ron writes the newsletter editorial and arranges for the preparation and mail of the newsletter to members.	5 hours per week
Chairman of the local management accounting group, where he also arranges speakers and venues for their meetings.	2 hours per month
Subcontracts to a superannuation auditor.	4–5 hours per week
Runs his own growing finance brokerage.	5.5 days per week
State treasurer for a state branch of the Australian Republican Movement.	8 hours per month
Lectures in accounting and computing (night classes).	3–4 hours per week
Conducts budgeting courses for real estate agents.	Varies

Conducts telemarketing campaigns for his finance business.	During day in the office
Tries to find time for at least one game of bowls and one game of golf per week.	Varies
Member of the Fellowship of Australian Writers and writes poetry in his spare time.	Varies

In addition to the above, Ron maintains their garden.

Ron and Fay also plan for a two-week holiday every two years, when they like to visit overseas islands.

SUMMARY:

In this chapter we . . .

- Examined the phenomenon known as the 'honeymoon period' of retirement.
- Looked at the beneficial effects of engaging in Purposeful Activities.
- Examined the principal reasons for involvement in Purposeful Activities.
- Examined the benefits of diversifying your Purposeful Activities.
- Listed a number of resources and strategies for finding Purposeful Activities that will suit your needs.

SECTION TWO

Maintaining and managing relationships

Maintaining effective and mutually supportive relationships with our partner, our adult children and our friends is important to our sense of wellbeing at any time in our lives. Once we have retired, the need for social interaction is further heightened by the fact that overnight we find ourselves removed from the social network previously provided by the workplace. At this time, retirement can also bring stresses due to the natural adjustment process that accompanies any significant life change. Relationships are then particularly important because being able to share with others what we are feeling, and how we are coping, is an important factor in the successful adjustment to our new lifestyle.

We also have a responsibility to 'be there' for our friends and relatives who may be experiencing their own dilemmas as they adjust to retirement.

Through the experiences of the 200 retirees who participated in the *Retire 200* research program, you will learn how the relationships of others were affected during retirement.

Five key areas of relationship management are discussed in this section of the book.

First, we will examine the important matter of communication within relationships. We will identify what is happening when communication fails and how we can take simple steps to improve it.

Second, we will see how, by using simply applied assertiveness skills, we can maximise the opportunities for obtaining our rights with a minimum of stress.

Third, we will look at how to handle the difficulties that can arise when conflict occurs between friends or neighbours. We will also examine the best ways to negotiate with business people when we are purchasing their goods or services.

Fourth, we will examine ways in which we can nurture and maintain our close relationships with our partner and others.

Finally, we will look at the importance of contributing and belonging once we have retired. With the social networks formerly provided by the workplace now severed, it becomes even more important for us to remain connected to our family and community.

It is hoped that these insights will be of assistance as you continue to improve aspects of your relationships that are presently not as satisfying as you would like them to be.

CHAPTER TWO

Communicating effectively within relationships

AIMS OF THIS CHAPTER

- To examine the importance of maintaining effective communication in your relationships.
- To learn new skills for improving the effectiveness of your communication style.
- To learn how to apply powerful listening skills.
- To learn how to manage the poor communication styles of others.

Why retirement may accentuate the effects of poor communication within relationships

We have all experienced how tense we become when, due to poor communication, things go wrong in our relationships. When we were in the workplace, we had the opportunity to allow an argument at home to dissipate as we threw ourselves into our work. Being separated during the day also allowed each partner the time and emotional space to cool off from an argument and, perhaps, to even start composing our apology (even if the disagreement was almost certainly the other partner's fault!). Once we have both retired, however, it is not as easy to 'escape' from each other, particularly if one of our post-retirement financial decisions has been to retain only one car that we share.

'We rarely talk to each other these days. If you are not happy then retirement won't cure it. Therefore get your relationship fixed up and get your priorities right.'

After years of being apart during the day, couples suddenly find themselves interacting at a personal level on just about everything they do. Consequently, those who have a solid relationship based on mutual respect and open communication will fare better than those for whom trust, respect, and communication are impoverished. The man quoted above sadly found that retirement placed insurmountable pressures on his already fragile relationship and, sadly, the couple parted soon after. Other couples found that even when their basic relationship was sound, communication could still break down under the special pressures brought about by retirement.

Being *seen* to communicate

There is an old saying that states, 'Justice must not only be done – it must be seen to be done.' Similar sentiments apply to the communication processes between partners and friends. As often as not, the real issue is not so much *what* is being said but *how* it is being conveyed. This is because communication involves more than just two people alternatively speaking and listening. Effective communication also involves the process of 'active listening'. When we listen actively we do not just 'hear' but are seen to be hearing by the way in which we physically and mentally attend to the other person.

Mary (hearing Steve arrive home)	*'Steve, guess what!'*
Steve (just noticing a bill on the table)	*'Uh! What?'*
Mary	*'I was elected president of the club today!'*
Steve (now horrified as he reads the 'bottom line' of the bill)	*'Uh! Oh! Good.'*
Mary (exasperated as she notes his distraction)	*'You haven't heard a thing I've just said!'*
Steve	*'Yes I did! You've just been made president of the club.'*

Did that type of exchange sound familiar? Steve 'heard' what Mary said. However, from Mary's perspective, their communication was not satisfying – he was not 'listening'. How many times have you been the victim or perpetrator of this type of impoverished communication? How did you feel when you were on the receiving end?

Sharing decision-making: consultation and communication with your partner

'I don't know why he didn't consult me on his choice of superannuation fund – he can't even balance his own chequebook! Now I find we've been locked in to a low-performing portfolio for twenty years.'

Financial problems can be a major source of relationship strain at *any* time of life. However, in retirement this is particularly true where finances may be limited to a fixed income. It is, therefore, important that partners discuss any financial plans and decisions that are going to significantly affect their lifestyle. When one-sided financial decisions impact negatively on retirement income, stress resulting from arguments over money is bound to occur. Just as important is the damage caused to the relationship where one partner feels devalued by their partner's poor consultation and its implicit lack of trust in their judgement. Even in relationships where one partner 'looks after the finances', it is still important to at least discuss what transactions are taking place and how they will affect living standards.

Improving communication in your relationships

Communicating your support for your partner's interests

'She is always complaining about me "wasting time mucking around in that stupid workshop" – what she doesn't understand is that since I have retired this hobby has become very important to my sanity – I need to be doing something.'

The changed circumstances created by retirement often increase the relevance of existing hobbies or interests. What was once a hobby involving a couple of hours here and there on a Saturday afternoon may become a daily activity replacing much of the sense of purpose and interest previously provided by the workplace. Yet a common complaint raised by participants of the *Retire 200* project occurred where someone failed to understand the importance of the activity to their partner. This situation caused unnecessary anxiety for some people who were made to feel guilty for wasting time or money on the pursuit of their pastime or interest.

The three most common reasons given for failing to recognise a partner's need to pursue their hobby were:

- Where the hobby or pastime was perceived by the other partner to lack a practical outcome, such as income from the sale of items produced in a workshop.
- Where financial resources were directed to the hobby at the expense of other priorities.
- Where the partner looking on suspected that their partner was primarily involved in the activity as a way of escaping from them!

If your partner resents the time you are spending on your pastime, you need to think carefully about how you are going to communicate to them why your activity is important to you. If you suspect that you are going to have difficulty with this communication, you may wish to consider the following points when explaining the importance of your pastime to your partner:

- 'It replaces some of the structure to my day previously provided by work.'
- 'It provides me with a reason to get up in the morning and feel enthusiastic.'
- 'Involvement in pastimes is my way of remaining mentally alert and physically fit.'
- 'Activity meets my need to be busy due to my work ethic.'
- 'My activity is fun! I enjoy it!'

How to maximise effective communication in relationships

There are two aspects of communication that are at the heart of most so-called 'communication breakdowns'. First, the *content* of what is being communicated is not fully understood by the listener. Poor communication of this type can be due to a number of reasons such as:

- The listener's lack of trust or respect for the speaker.
- The listener's preconceived view of what the speaker 'really' means.
- Not listening attentively due to lack of interest in the topic.

Second, but just as important, is the *style* or tone of interpersonal communication we use. Interestingly, the closer we are to someone, the more dysfunctional our chosen communication style may be! Using poor styles such as 'talking down' to our partner can result in resentment and anger that can seriously damage a relationship. It is, therefore, important that we get it right.

In the next section of this chapter, we will start by looking at the skills we need to use to communicate accurately and effectively with our partner and friends.

Listening – the hardest part of effective communication!

Let me warn you now: if you become skilled in this difficult aspect of communicating, you may find that people who want to pour out their hearts will regularly besiege you! Genuine Active Listening, the type that psychologists are paid for, is easy to describe and easy to understand in theory, but exhaustingly difficult to put into practice.

The reason that effective communication can be so demanding is that it involves the use of a number of communication skills at once. As these skills do not usually come naturally to most people, they take considerable practice to master. However, if you are determined to put in the work on your interpersonal communication skills, you *will* see results.

Notwithstanding the hard work associated with learning and applying effective communication skills, there are times in every relationship where it is of the utmost importance to both listen and to be heard. To further complicate matters, it is sometimes important to communicate most effectively at the very time when effective communication is at its most difficult to achieve! An example could be where there is an emotional issue affecting you both, such as the unexpected terminal illness of a close mutual friend. Remaining calm and objectively discussing how you can both assist your friend will be more difficult if you have trouble communicating under normal circumstances.

How to listen 'actively'

Remember how Mary reacted to Steve when he read the bill while she was trying to celebrate her good news? How many times have *you* heard someone say, 'You are not listening to me!' Were you doing something else – such as fiddling with something or daydreaming while the person was speaking or were you just conveying the impression that you were bored? The process of 'active listening' vastly improves such poor communication.

The acronym S-O-L-E-R is sometimes used to describe the high level of active listening skills used in counselling. Effective communication involves the listener attending to all of the following processes. If you become skilled in these communication skills, you will find that you, and those with whom you are communicating, will benefit enormously.

Face the person Squarely

Have you noticed how pleasant it is when someone you are talking to turns towards you to listen? You feel as if they are absorbing and valuing what you say. On the other hand, we have all experienced situations where a bored shop assistant takes your food order while they grumpily wipe down a counter. It does not leave you with much confidence that you will get what you ordered!

Use an Open posture

There is no need to be fanatical about this step. For example, it is quite okay to sit with your legs crossed if this is more comfortable. However, folding your arms across your chest should be avoided, as this behaviour may be interpreted as you reacting in a judgemental or defensive manner.

*L*ean towards the person

Leaning forward a little indicates to the other person that you are interested in what they are saying. You will notice people who are discussing an interesting topic sometimes lean forward as they become animated. This may be where the saying 'I was sitting on the edge of my seat!' comes from. On the other hand, getting very comfortable and sliding down in your chair in a reclining or slouching manner can indicate that you are more interested in your own comfort than in what the other person is saying.

Maintain appropriate *E*ye contact

Maintaining appropriate eye contact indicates to the other person that you are attending to them. This does not mean fixing them with an unrelenting, steely-eyed stare but, rather, maintaining regular eye contact. On the other hand, gazing out the window or picking at a loose thread on your clothing indicates pretty clearly that you are not focusing on what they are saying.

*R*elax

Before you start the communication process, think about how you are presenting yourself. Are you acting tensely, or indicating that you do not approve of the person? If so, communication will certainly break down. Get yourself reasonably comfortable and then attend to all of the above aspects of communication covered by S-O-L-E-R.

If the above skills are to become an effective part of your communication repertoire, you will need to practise them and then use them regularly.

'Listening' to non-verbal language (body language)

There has been a lot of nonsense written about body language in 'pop' psychology books. Some people would have you believe that you can read a person's mind simply by watching how they sit, whether they scratch the left side of their nose or the right, and so on. This is not to say that body language – or non-verbal language, as it is correctly termed – does not provide valuable insights into what a person is communicating when they speak. The real key to interpreting non-verbal behaviour is to look at the *context* in which it appears. For example, if I sit down and fold my arms it could be for any one of the following reasons:

- I have just come in from a blustering winter's wind and I am cold.
- I may be feeling defensive and threatened by the topic being discussed.
- I may have a pain in my back that is relieved by sitting with my arms folded.
- I may be trying to hide the stain on my shirt where mayonnaise dripped on it at lunchtime.

An example of interpreting non-verbal language in context could be where I am sitting in an open posture and then suddenly fold my arms if someone accuses me of doing something unpleasant. Here it is reasonable to suspect that I am feeling defensive (but not necessarily guilty!).

Non-verbal behaviour should also be congruent with, and consequently confirm, what is being said. For example, if I were to say, 'I've never felt so happy and carefree' while frowning sternly, you would need to ask more questions to see which one of the conflicting messages was correct!

Listening to verbal language

When people communicate with you, they will do so at the three levels shown below:

1. Their experiences

The person you are communicating with will tell you *what* is happening that is affecting their lives.

> *'Last night I heard a loud noise in the backyard.'*

2. Their behaviours

The person you are communicating with will tell you about their *actions/behaviours.*

> *'I got out of bed as quietly as I could and peeped through the curtains to see if I could work out what had made the noise.'*

3. Their feelings

The person you are communicating with will tell you how they *are feeling* either physically and/or emotionally.

> *'My heart was pounding and I felt very scared.'*

While you will find that people will frequently tell you *what* happened to them (experiences), and *how* they reacted (behaviours), they frequently leave it to you to gauge how they *felt* because to them it appears so obvious. An experienced counsellor realises at this point that it is important to seek clarification by saying something like,

> *'How did you feel about that?' or 'Were you very upset?'*

Further questions are then used to identify what it was about the event that caused them the most anguish. The following example demonstrates a number of possible reactions to the same event.

> *'Yesterday, I tripped over in the city. As I fell, I tore my new slacks. A group of teenage boys on skateboards just looked at me and laughed while I lay there stunned. Eventually a young couple helped me up. I was so upset that I came straight back home without doing any shopping. I felt awful!'*

Depending on your own perspective you could easily jump to a number of conclusions as to why the person was upset. Doing so, by applying your own values, could put you way off target. Here are some possible reasons for your friend/partner being upset:

- The slacks were new and cost a lot of money.
- They found being laughed at embarrassing.
- They were concerned by the callous behaviour of the young skateboarders and the possible implications of where society was headed.
- It was frightening to consider that they may have broken a bone or hip.
- They may have lost some confidence and were now fearful of falling again.

However, the only way you can find out what *really* upset them is to ask questions.

Responding to people so that they feel 'listened to'

When a skilled professional is listening to you, they will use a number of methods to signal to you that they are both hearing and understanding what you are saying. Here are a few techniques they use which you can put into action.

1. Gestures

Nodding and gesturing with your hand for the person to continue talking while you remain silent indicates that you are focusing on what they are saying, and that you wish them to continue without interruption.

2. Minimal encouragers

Verbal responses such as 'Mm-hm' and 'Uh-huh' are known as minimal encouragers. Minimal encouragers motivate the person to continue talking yet contain no judgemental message that could stop the communication flow. When people are upset or embarrassed, even comparatively innocent phrases such as 'I see' can be interpreted as casting a negative judgement on what the person is saying. For example:

'Then I'm afraid I lost my temper and threw a glass at him.'

'Uh-huh' (rather than 'I see!')

3. Asking for clarification

When someone is upset they may be talking to you through tears, or in a confused state of mind. If you are finding it hard to follow what they are saying, or if you have temporarily lost concentration, always seek clarification. It will demonstrate to them that you care about understanding them properly and will also reduce the likelihood of you misinterpreting the content. For example:

'I don't quite understand – what did he do after you threw the glass at him?'

4. Paraphrasing

Paraphrasing – that is, repeating what someone has said to you using your own words – is an extremely powerful way of demonstrating that you are listening attentively. It also verifies whether you have correctly understood the meaning behind what they have said. If you find that you have misunderstood the content of their message, they will usually tell you quickly!

'After I threw the glass at him I broke down and cried.'

'So when you threw the glass you felt silly?'

'No! I felt angry and hurt!'

5. Accenting key phrases

When people are relating the details of an event or feeling that is affecting them, they may do so in a jumble of words and sentences that are disjointed, or distorted by sobs, as they relive the experience. It is important that you let them do most of the talking so that they can get it all out. An effective way of letting them know you are following the important parts of their message is just to echo the key words or phrases that you believe are at the core of their communication:

'Then he walked out saying that he was never coming back.'

'Never *coming back?'*

'That's right! I couldn't believe that I was hearing it!'

Managing poor communication styles (yours and others')

'My husband can be so overbearing at times. I ordered some sandwiches for us in the coffee shop the other day. When they arrived, he dressed me down in front of the waitress for not asking for wholemeal bread! I felt like a child.'

Back in 1961, Dr Eric Berne wrote a book called *Transactional Analysis in Psychotherapy.* It was the forerunner to his successful book *The Games People Play.* In a similar vein, Dr Thomas Harris's book *I'm OK – You're OK* followed a short time later.

For a while, Transactional Analysis, or TA, was all the rage in psychiatric and psychological settings. It was taught in counselling classes around the world and teachers learned its fundamentals in postgraduate teacher training courses. At an organisational level, TA became the subject of courses run by human resources consultants. Like many ideas that become popular, it was eventually viewed as a fad and later fell out of fashion in mainstream psychology.

However, when it comes to identifying poor communication styles, TA remains a relatively easy concept for people without formal counselling training to apply. It enables the quick recognition of inappropriate communication styles, and, just as importantly, provides a structure for dealing with annoying communication styles where *you* are on the receiving end.

What follows now is an introduction to Transactional Analysis. I hope it is as helpful to you as it has been for my clients and me.

Transactional Analysis (TA) explained

According to TA, people are described as using one of three modes of communication, namely, Parent (P), Adult (A), or Child (C). TA practitioners argue that effective communication most often occurs when we are using the Adult mode.

So how do the modes differ?

1. Parent mode [judgemental, interfering]

When we are communicating in Parent mode, we may use the following verbal and non-verbal (body language) styles.

The way 'Parents' look	The way 'Parents' speak
Arms folded	*'Now look here!'*
Hands on the hips	*'If I were you I would . . .'*
Frowning (for impact)	*'Why are you always so late? Now we are going to keep Jenny waiting.'*
Sighing with exasperation	*'Don't ask questions – just do it!'*

Are you ever on the receiving end of this type of communication? Stop and reflect for a moment about occasions when you have experienced the Parent communication style. How does it make you feel?

Do you ever dish out this type of communication to others? In what sort of settings are you likely to do this?

2. Child mode [childish, immature]

When we are communicating in Child mode, we may use the following verbal and non-verbal (body language) styles.

The way the 'Child' looks	The way the 'Child' speaks
Tears	*'I wish, I want . . .'*
Shrugging	*Overuse of superlatives – that is, the 'mine-is-better' game*
Whining	*'Gee, do I have to?'*
Displays of bad temper, sulking	*'I don't care'*

Do you ever behave in this way? Most people do from time to time! Under what circumstances are you likely to do this?

3. Adult mode [mature, intelligent]

When we are in Adult mode, we use the following verbal and non-verbal (body language) styles.

The way the 'Adult' looks	The way the 'Adult' speaks
Facial and body movements indicate non-judgemental listening	*'Who? What? Where? When? How?'*
Calm – concentrating on the interaction	*'I think that is right . . .'*
	'In my opinion . . .'

How often do people treat you like an adult during communication? Stop and reflect for a moment on some examples that you have experienced. How does this style of communication make you feel?

Here are some examples of combinations of Parent, Child, and Adult interactions:

Child–Parent interaction

Husband to wife	*'Please let me watch the football – you know how much I love it. I'll cut the grass tomorrow.' (Child)*

Parent–Child interaction

Wife to husband	*'Go and cut the grass first then you can watch all the TV you like.' (Parent)*

Do these styles of interactions sound familiar? They are generally not satisfying for either party.

Parent–Parent interactions

Sue to Jane	*'Mary looks ridiculous in that short dress – she's no spring chicken.' (Parent)*
Jane to Sue	*'Oh, she is always wearing outfits like that! She's no supermodel.' (Parent)*

Child–Child interactions

John to Mary	*'I want to get that new TV – I've got to have it!' (Child)*
Mary to John	*'But I want to buy that ring I showed you the other day.' (Child)*

Adult–Adult interactions

Husband to wife	*'I think I will watch the football now.'*
Wife to husband	*'When do you plan to cut the grass? It's getting pretty long.'*

Okay, so what does all this mean? How can we use this information to improve communication in our own relationships?

Essentially, when people respond in Child or Parent modes, they are attempting to get their own way in an emotionally laden and unintelligent way. For example, imagine that you need to take an afternoon off from your part-time job to attend to an important personal matter. You talk to the boss and the conversation goes like this:

> *'Ian, I have an important personal matter to attend to next Thursday afternoon. Do you mind if I take that afternoon off?' (Adult)*

'Look, Mary, can't you see how busy we are? If you don't want to work there are plenty of others who would like your job.' (Parent)

That was not very satisfactory, was it? Nobody was satisfied there. Mary would have felt humiliated and resentful because her needs were ignored. Her boss, Ian, may also reflect later that he could have handled the situation better. From his point of view, it hardly demonstrated good management practice.

So what do you do when you are confronted with a response like that? For many people, their first response is to fire back an answer in either Child or Parent mode. Here is an example:

'Oh, go on, Ian! You know what I good girl I am and how hard I always work for you!' (Child)

Interestingly, this may just work! However, how satisfying is it for Mary? Do you think she would then feel valued as a mature, intelligent woman? Is this the way an enlightened manager should encourage staff to act?

Here is an example of Mary responding to Ian in Parent mode:

'Look, you may be the boss but that is no way to treat people – how dare you be so inconsiderate.' (Parent)

Responding to the communication of others with Parent mode communication is how disputes often start. Such communication might make you feel good at the time but it gets nowhere until someone backs off.

What is the solution?

The ideal way to respond to the demanding Parent or the whining Child is to use the Adult mode. You may find that the other person continues in their Parent or Child mode for a time. However, if you ignore this behaviour and persist in using the Adult mode, you will increase your chances of establishing effective communication. Here is an example using the 'Mary and Ian' scenario again.

> *'Ian, I have a personal matter to attend to next Thursday afternoon. Do you mind if I take that afternoon off?' (Adult)*
>
> *'Look, Mary, can't you see how busy we are? If you don't want to work there are plenty of others who would like your job.' (Parent)*
>
> *'Yes, Ian – I realise we are busy but I do need the time off.' (Adult)*
>
> *'Give me a break, Mary – you don't want me to lose my job, do you?' (Child)*
>
> *'Ian, it is very important that I take the time off on Thursday – can we discuss a way for me to make up the time – say, this Saturday morning?' (Adult)*
>
> *'Well, okay, if you put in a couple of hours on Saturday we would still get the order out by our Tuesday deadline.' (Adult)*

OR

> *'Mary, we have to meet our deadline by Friday night – I am afraid it is just not possible to give you time off this week. Perhaps there is a way for you to change your Thursday appointment?' (Adult)*

As you can see from the above, you may not always get your way. However, the communication is effective and everyone concerned is treated like an adult of intelligence and substance. Mary held her ground by being assertive and maintaining an Adult communication mode, and her boss finally 'grew up' and behaved accordingly.

Why does using the Adult mode improve communication?

- First, if you persist in using the Adult mode in the face of the whining Child or the overbearing Parent you will hear yourself speaking as a reasonable and intelligent person. This does wonders for your self-esteem.
- Second, the annoying behaviour of the other person is eventually more likely to diminish as they hear themselves responding in an inappropriate way when compared to your reasonable, mature communication style.

Attitudinal impediments to your ability to communicate

In the two sections above we examined communication skills and how to manage dysfunctional communication styles. However, it does not matter how skilled you are if your attitude is not right.

Below are five attitudinal issues to get right before starting effective communication.

1. How you are feeling

If you are not feeling well, or are presently anxious due to your own personal concerns, you may not be able to provide the high levels of energy needed to communicate effectively. If this is the case, you should let the person you are communicating with know your situation. Suggest to them that you meet with them later so that you can give them your full attention and assistance.

2. Their issue = your issue

The topic they may wish to discuss may also be a highly charged issue for you. For example, if your friend is upset because a newspaper article has brought back sad or disturbing memories, and you also find that the article triggers similar emotions in you, point this out early in the conversation.

3. Enthusiasm

When people are anxious to help or to please, they may only hear half of what the other person is saying and leap in, assuming they know how the person was going to complete their sentence. It is not helpful to do this for two important reasons:

- If you get it wrong you will annoy the other person because they will have to start their story all over again. This may be distressing for them if the topic under discussion is affecting them strongly.
- Even if you are correct, you are denying them the opportunity to talk matters over and to get the issues off their chest.

4. Preoccupation with your own problems

It is very difficult to attend to another person's problems when there is something bothering you. For example, if you were waiting for a pathology report which will determine whether or not you have a serious illness, it is very difficult to empathise with someone who is complaining about a bad cold.

5. Defensive listening

Think back to a time when you have had to tell someone something that you knew would annoy or anger them. For example, imagine that you and your partner bought a new car six weeks ago. Today, on your way home from lunch with a friend, you scrape the side of the car as you pull out of a tight parking space. This is the second time in twelve months that you have had such an accident and you suspect that your partner feels that the first accident was due to your carelessness. As you drive home and contemplate the conversation to come, you may feel yourself becoming defensive. You 'know' what your partner is going to say!

Unfortunately, defensiveness is one of the most common impediments to effective communication. Just as a safe environment, in which there is approval and acceptance, will encourage us to continue talking, a negative, judgemental, and evaluative environment blocks effective communication. Therefore, to help keep your own communication open and honest, when you believe someone may be feeling defensive about a topic, try the following steps.

1. BE POSITIVE TO THE PERSON

Try to separate your reaction to the *content* of what the person is saying from your reaction to them as a person. For instance, in the case of the scratched car, it would be helpful if the partner listening to the story said something like:

> *'This is very annoying – you must be upset.'*

By saying this, the message conveyed is:

> *'I am annoyed that the car is damaged, but I am not annoyed with you.'*

It also acknowledges your empathy for their feelings and embarrassment.

2. WAIT BEFORE YOU EVALUATE

If you are finding the content of someone's communication annoying, it can be tempting to cut them off or to leap in with a sarcastic remark, for example:

> *'Where did you think you were driving – in the grand prix?'*

It is wiser to hold back before you evaluate and let the other person get their story out in an atmosphere of trust and mutual respect. Wait until you have heard the *complete* story (and until you have calmed down if this is relevant), before making any premature or damning comments. In other words, create the type of environment *you* would want if the boot were on the other foot!

3. MINIMISE YOUR NEGATIVE EVALUATIONS AND FEELINGS

As the other person is relating the story, try to minimise any tendency to tune in selectively to the negative, punitive aspects of the event. In the example of the car accident, you might find yourself imagining your partner driving in a careless or erratic manner when, in fact, nothing may be further from the truth.

4. ENCOURAGE THE PERSON TO CONTINUE EVEN IF YOU ARE BECOMING ANNOYED

Encourage the other person to speak freely and openly. If you find yourself getting angry or upset, breathe deeply and slowly. It is probably much harder for them to discuss the topic than it is for you to listen.

A footnote: Love, familiarity, and intimacy – blocks to communication

It sounds crazy, doesn't it? How can intimacy be an obstacle to effective communication? Yet a common communication trap that people in close relationships fall for is relying on the romantic notion that because they are in love, communication should not need to be worked at. Consequently, partners may operate on the flawed premise that 'he/she ought to know how I feel on this subject' and leave the hard work of effective communication to chance. It seems that many of us have two sets of rules when it comes to interpersonal communication: one for their spouse or partner and the other for communication with everyone else!

SUMMARY:
In this chapter we . . .

- Examined how adjusting to life in retirement can bring special pressures on relationships in which communication is poor.
- Learned how to apply active listening when communicating with others.
- Differentiated verbal listening from non-verbal (body language) listening.
- Examined the model of interpersonal communication known as Transactional Analysis.
- Identified attitudinal impediments to effective communication.

CHECKLIST

- ☐ I will try not to communicate as an overbearing 'Parent' or as a whining 'Child'.
- ☐ I will attend to the communications of others by using appropriate non-verbal (body language) communication to support my verbal responses.
- ☐ I will work hard to create an environment where open and effective communication is encouraged.
- ☐ I will try not to react defensively to criticism or bad news.

CHAPTER THREE

Assertiveness skills – getting your rights without stress

AIMS OF THIS CHAPTER

- To discuss the need for assertiveness skills in retirement.
- To understand how assertive, non-assertive, and aggressive behaviours differ.
- To describe how to use assertive behaviour to achieve your rights without causing yourself unnecessary stress.

What is assertiveness?

What do you think of when you hear the word 'assertive'? Do you picture someone pushing and shoving their way to the top of a queue? Do you imagine a shopper barking commands at a shop assistant? In fact, both of these situations are examples of 'aggression' where the person involved gets their way at the expense of someone else's rights or feelings. At the other end of the scale, but just as ineffective, is non-assertive behaviour whereby you give up your rights out of fear or lack of confidence.

Assertiveness, however, is the calm, reasonable process of establishing and then requesting what is rightfully yours. Such rights may range from fair and equitable treatment in a relationship to the respect and service you deserve from the staff of your bank, irrespective of the size of your account balance!

Below is an example that demonstrates how aggressive, non-assertive, and assertive behaviours differ in style. For the example, let us say that your cousin has heard that you have a new camera and approaches you to borrow it to use during his annual holiday interstate. You have paid a lot of money for the camera and you do not wish to lend it to anyone. What is more, your cousin has a poor record when it comes to looking after other people's property.

You could respond in three ways:

Style of behaviour	Example of response
Aggressive	*'Don't be ridiculous! Of course you can't borrow my new camera – I paid a lot of money for it and I don't want it broken.'*
Non-assertive	*'Well, I don't like lending expensive things such as this but if you promise to be careful with it I suppose it is all right.'*

Style of behaviour	Example of response
Assertive	*'John, I'd rather not – the camera is too expensive to lend out.'*

If assertiveness is that easy, why aren't all people assertive?

There are many reasons for people not acting assertively and, not surprisingly, these vary from person to person. Here are some examples.

Reasons people use non-assertive behaviour

- *They may suffer from low self-esteem and self-confidence:* When people have low self-esteem or self-confidence, they will often devalue their own rights, believing that the needs of others are more important. As a consequence, they may make comments like:

  'But what will they think of me?'
  'Am I being unreasonable?'
  'I'll only get tongue-tied or embarrassed!'
  'There are other people waiting to be served and I am holding them up.'

- *They may have a fear of conflict:* Many people simply find the prospect of conflict too stressful. If their need to avoid conflict is high, they may simply give up their rights to avoid a stressful situation.
- *They lack the necessary assertiveness skills:* Many people have not seen assertive behaviour applied skilfully before. For example, if as a child they saw their parents deal with unacceptable behaviour with either non-assertive or aggressive behaviours, this may become 'normal' behaviour for them too.

Reasons people use aggressive behaviour

When an item we buy turns out to be faulty, it is common to go through a range of emotions. Where people respond aggressively, it can be due to any of the following reasons:

- *They may be confusing the person with the problem:* For example, abusing an employee of a large chain store because a product purchased there is faulty:

  'Here we go again – why is it that every time I buy something these days there is something wrong with it?!'

  By the time the customer gets back to the place of purchase, they may end up venting their frustration on the first person who serves them instead of focusing their attention on the faulty product or service. Of course, in many cases the problem is not the fault of the person who sold us the product, yet if we are annoyed and inconvenienced they can become an easy scapegoat for our frustration.
- *Embarrassment:* Sometimes people whose usual demeanour is meek will attempt to mask their lack of assertiveness skills by becoming aggressive. Unfortunately, they can then become so wound up due to their level of anxiety that they risk storming out of the store without achieving their aim.
- *Low tolerance for frustration:* Some people are simply emotionally immature and have a correspondingly low tolerance for frustration. When things go wrong for such people, it may bring on an emotional outburst. This could be anything from a slow-moving queue at the supermarket to the more serious issue of road rage when someone's driving behaviour annoys them.

Assertive behaviour in relationships

Spouse/partner relationships

As the date of retirement draws nearer, most people find themselves starting to imagine what their new lifestyle will be like. Discussions may centre around their plans for leisure activities, on 'the trip around Australia', or on drawing up budgets for maximising their lifestyles on a fixed income. However, very few people sit down before retirement and discuss the important subject of their need for individual space and autonomy. Consequently, when the first day of retirement arrives, one partner may be expecting a lifestyle involving the emotional space to 'do their own thing' while the other partner may be envisaging a lifestyle where they do most things together. Clearly, these differing expectations need to be resolved if both people are to live mutually fulfilling lives; assertive behaviour is sometimes required to achieve this outcome.

Relationships with friends and acquaintances

Friends are important partly because they usually know you better than most others do; they may also be your link to important events and memories from years ago. Yet close friends may feel that they can take liberties with you that others would not dream of taking. For example, an old friend who needs a golfing partner each Tuesday may expect you to fill that role even though they know that you would rather play less frequently. Consequently, you need to ensure that you assertively maintain your rights while still preserving old and irreplaceable friendships.

The top five relationship issues raised by the *Retire 200*

Participants on the *Retire 200* research identified five important areas that they felt required the skilful use of assertive behaviour to manage potential relationship problems.

1. Having your own space

'Husbands and wives should not live in each other's pockets – they need to have some interests apart, some time to themselves.'

Getting a partner to understand the importance to you of having physical and emotional space can take time and effort to achieve. For many people, this 'space' involves having a dedicated room in the house in which they pursue hobbies or interests with minimal disruption. For others, it is an office or workshop.

'Create your own space – don't annoy your partner – live independently from them to a degree.'

A number of people complained that when they expressed their need for some time alone, their partner would become offended and interpret the request as their partner being tired of them! In particular, women found it annoying when their husband 'follows me around the house all day!' Another common issue arose where bored husbands volunteered to drive their wives to social engagements. The problem here is that by picking up their wife at a previously arranged time, they restrict their wife's freedom to act spontaneously and to choose how long they will stay at these events.

Note: The behaviours described above are sometimes referred to in sociological literature as 'the underfoot husband' phenomenon.

While the need to have their own space is usually resolved during the first twelve months of retirement, some people reported that working through the issue was not always easy. Misunderstandings, and even mistrust, sometimes got in the way of intelligent, orderly discussion; being able to assert one's rights skilfully was important at this time. A clear balance needs to be struck between giving up some rights to keep the peace, and asserting the right to have appropriate periods of time to oneself.

2. Being free to 'do your own thing'

'I retired to keep my older retired husband company (at his insistence). I now do two hours' voluntary work a week – I would like to do much more than this but my husband won't let me.'

I guess that many of you who have just read the above quote are now bristling with indignation. How could someone be so unreasonable! However, this story actually gets worse: sadly, the woman quoted above indicated that she felt so constricted by her husband's demands, and was so resentful about her plight, that she claimed she was losing the will to live.

The powerful desire for freedom of activity relates to our strongly entrenched need as adults to be independent, and to resent having our lives overly controlled. In the above example, this woman's lack of ability to skilfully assert her rights was not just annoying but had become potentially a matter of life and death.

3. Not being taken for granted

'Have a life of your own – don't be an "on-call" babysitter.'

While many people welcome the role of babysitter, others do not. Some people complained that their adult children made them feel guilty by citing how hard working life was 'these days'. While manipulation of this type is obviously not acceptable, the fact remains that with child-minding costs escalating and couples working to pay off large mortgages, retired parents can be viewed as a convenient unpaid creche.

'I have four adult children, three sons and one daughter. One morning last year "good old Nana" found that she had six children to babysit that day. All were under the age of eight – by the time their parents collected them later that evening I was completely exhausted. At the age of sixty-two it was me who spat the dummy!'

Where more than one adult child has children, some people described being forced to put their babysitting services on a roster simply because they could not cope with looking after all of their grandchildren at once. Relationships became strained when grandparents found themselves in the difficult situation of having to choose which of their grandchildren to babysit on a particular day. Insult was added to injury when, rather than being grateful for their retired parent's services, some adult children attempted to pressure them into taking the grandchildren more frequently.

Many of these problems could have been avoided through the application of appropriate assertiveness on the part of the retired grandparents, and some empathy on the part of their adult children. We will look at ways of being assertive in valued relationships, without creating World War III, later in this chapter.

4. Dealing with well-meaning friends and relatives who interfere

'Tell people who want you to do things to get lost – do your own thing – retain your independence.'

'Please yourself – don't act to meet others' expectations.'

There is nothing more infuriating than for an adult to be told what is good for them or that 'what you should do is . . .' It can be even harder to bite your tongue when well-meaning people offer you unsolicited advice when you are going through a period of significant change. Effective assertiveness skills are necessary to ensure that you impress upon well-meaning family and friends that retirement is *your* time to do what you like.

'Don't let others tell you what to do.'

One of the first lessons a first-year psychology student receives in 'Counselling 101' is that *telling* people how to run their lives and how to solve their problems is a waste of time. The fact is that if personal problem-solving was that easy, someone would have written the *Solutions to Life's Problems* manual years ago and would now be sitting back counting their millions. Offering unsolicited advice, no matter how well meaning, simply does not work because adults prefer to work through their own problems.

When attempts to resolve one's problems do not work, professional assistance from a psychologist or skilled counsellor can help. The psychologist/counsellor then acts as a facilitator who, rather than just suggesting a solution to the problem, provides the structure and objective feedback required to assist the person to arrive at a workable solution. Moreover, a secondary objective of professional counselling is to provide the client with a problem-solving model or process which they can then apply to future problems.

5. Ending relationships – 'What? At my time of life!'

'Many people continue to drift along in dead or even violent relationships because they are fearful of leaving the relationship. "What would people think?" they ask.'

We are all familiar with stories of people staying in unsatisfactory marriages for 'the sake of the children'. Even then, it is sometimes difficult to understand why your friend puts up with the ongoing hell they experience in their relationship. Clearly, it is a complicated area with few simple solutions.

It is tempting to imagine that by the time retirement comes along, most dysfunctional relationships would either have been sorted out or dissolved. Yet approximately 20 per cent of those people participating in the *Retire 200* research program were not happy in their relationships (of course, this means that 80 per cent *were* happy, which is probably a better way to view it!). The reasons given for persevering with poor relationships were many and varied. Here are some of their comments:

'We both have our own interests so we hardly ever see each other.'

'We could not break up now! What would our children and friends think?'

'I have had a lover now for nearly twenty years – my husband does not know and I doubt whether he would care even if he found out.'

'We would both like to separate but we cannot afford to.'

'We did divorce some fifteen years ago but then remarried due to loneliness. Both of our marriages were mistakes!'

Deciding whether to remain in an unsatisfactory relationship is a complex process. Even when both parties are keen to separate, issues regarding finance and accommodation are important when income is typically less than it was when they were in the workforce.

For those of you reading this book and contemplating separation, it may be wise to seek professional advice from someone who is experienced in relationship counselling. The goal of professional relationship counsellors (once called marriage guidance counsellors), is not to preserve the relationship 'at all costs'. Relationship counsellors will work to help you to identify and clarify the realities of your specific situation. The aim of the process is then for you both to arrive at a more objective assessment of whether your relationship is worth salvaging or not. Where it is, some change is usually required by both parties to repair the damage caused by previous dysfunctional behaviours.

Irrespective of whether you repair a flawed relationship or ultimately decide to end it, your ability to assert your rights is important. If you stay together, assertiveness will be required to ensure that any agreed changes in behaviour actually take place and persist. If you separate, assertive behaviour will be required to attend to matters such as arranging new accommodation and ensuring that property is distributed equitably.

Ways to improve your assertiveness skills

Asserting your rights in relationships

Assertive behaviour is simply the act of expressing our desires and needs openly and honestly. Here is an example that demonstrates the difference between assertive, non-assertive, and aggressive behaviours.

☑ Assertive behaviour	*'I would like to borrow the car on Wednesday so that I can visit our grandchildren.'*
☒ Aggressive behaviour	*'I'm going to borrow the car on Wednesday whether you like it or not. If you kick up a fuss about it, you can do your own cooking for the rest of the week.'*
☒ Non-assertive behaviour	*'May I borrow the car on Wednesday – that is, if you don't think it is possible that you may want it yourself?'*

When you are being assertive, it is not just a matter of using the right words. You also need to use assertive *non-verbal* behaviour (body language), to support your spoken language. Below is a list of behaviours that assertive people use – the non-assertive and aggressive equivalents are also shown for comparison.

☑ **Assertive Behaviour**	☒ **Non-assertive Behaviour**	☒ **Aggressive Behaviour**
Making eye contact to demonstrate that you mean what you say.	Looking away, or at your feet, when speaking.	Glaring and staring nastily.
Facing people squarely.	Turning your body away or moving back when speaking.	Moving quickly to the person, invading their personal space (getting too close), wagging your finger at them.
Matching facial expressions with the content of the message	Using inappropriate expressions – for example, looking apologetic when requesting something that is your right.	Using inappropriate expressions – for example, frowning threateningly.
Speaking with appropriate volume.	Whispering or mumbling.	Yelling, screaming.
Using active-case 'I' statements – for example, 'I would like you to help me tidy up the house before our friends arrive.'	Using passive-case statements – for example, 'It would be nice if the house could be tidied up before our friends arrive.'	Getting personal – for example, 'Tidy up the house. I am sick and tired of your sloppy ways.'

Knowing what comprises assertiveness is one thing – actually being assertive is another! People who have difficulty with assertive behaviour usually know what they would *like* to say – doing it can be a different matter.

Rehearsing to be assertive

How, then, can you develop the skills you need to express your feelings, and to get your rights in relationships? One solution frequently used by psychologists is to teach their clients the technique of behavioural rehearsal. Here is how it works:

Step 1

Think of an issue that is bothering you because you have not assertively addressed it with the person involved. If you cannot think of an issue, make one up for the purpose of the exercise. For example:

> *'Since we have retired my husband and I have had Sue and Mike around for dinner three times in a row, yet they keep on coming around without any apparent intention of returning our hospitality. I find that I am getting resentful, and it is starting to affect how I feel about Sue. If I don't raise the issue with her soon, this resentment will get worse.'*

Step 2

Plan how you will approach Sue in a socially acceptable yet assertive manner. For example:

> *'Sue, John and I were saying the other day that we have not been around to your place for dinner for ages. Why don't we get together soon? I have lots to tell you.'*

You may be wondering why you do not say something like:

> *'Sue, John and I were saying the other night that we can't understand why it is that despite us having you around*

> *for dinner three times in a row, you have never returned the invitation!'*

There are two reasons for using the first approach with Sue:

- First, your friends Sue and Mike may genuinely believe that accepting three consecutive dinners at your place does not constitute unreasonable behaviour and may be planning to invite you to their home for the next dinner.
- Second, as they are friends, the goal of the exercise is to be diplomatically assertive while retaining the friendship.

Some psychologists refer to this diplomacy as using the 'minimal effective response' technique – that is, achieving your desired outcome without unwanted side effects.

Using the minimal effective response technique is also a good idea when dealing with awkward issues with a neighbour. For example, saying something like the following is assertive, but probably inappropriate:

> *'I have consulted the by-laws officer and he tells me that under Section 234 (i) (a), I have the right to have your dog destroyed if it continues to bark at night. Please rectify the situation immediately.'*

Step 3

Having selected an issue with which to rehearse your assertive behaviours, design or script your statement. Use some of the examples described above to get some ideas for how to structure your approach.

Practise your delivery aloud in front of a mirror. Alternatively, you can ask your partner or a friend to role-play with you, or you could go through this exercise with a psychologist if you are seeing one.

By rehearsing aloud, or with a 'coach' present, you give yourself the opportunity to hear what your communication would sound like. You can then adjust your choice of words, timing or manner of speech according to what you hear yourself saying, or according to the advice of your coach.

While you are rehearsing, remember to also attend to your assertive non-verbal behaviours (body language), which were described earlier in this chapter.

Not all attempts at assertiveness will be perfect

Just as rehearsals for a play or a concert do not always result in perfect performances, you may find that some people respond to your assertive behaviour with rudeness, or by just ignoring your request. There is no need for you then to feel that you have failed. You have already done well simply by demonstrating your desire to assert your rights.

Remember, there are *two* goals of assertive behaviour:

1. To assert your desire for your rights to be respected (for your self-esteem).
2. To achieve your rights.

Even where people choose not to act on your requests, or where they meet your approach with rudeness, you will still have achieved the goal of establishing and requesting your rights. This in itself is important for your continued self-esteem and establishes that you are someone who is prepared to stand up for themselves.

Sometimes it is very important to obtain your rights and not all of the people you approach will welcome your request – particularly where they have a strong emotional or financial interest in preserving the status quo. Where you encounter such resistance, you can try the following strategies:

Assertiveness strategies for specific situations

1. Assertively using distraction to prevent someone from discussing your personal affairs

If someone is moving the topic of the conversation to a personal matter that you do not wish to discuss, try using distraction:

> *'You mentioned before that since you have retired you have set up a workshop under your house. What sort of things do you make there?'*
>
> or
>
> *'I hear you have been overseas recently. How did you enjoy the trip?'*

2. Assertively changing the subject when you are not comfortable with the topic

A friend who is visiting you may start discussing details of a terminal illness that a friend is suffering from. You feel that continued discussion of the topic will be upsetting. Your assertive response could be:

> *'Anne, that subject is a little upsetting – I would rather talk about something else, if you don't mind.'*
>
> or
>
> *'Anne, do you mind if we discuss something else?'*

3. Assertively winding up an inappropriate or boring conversation

You can start by using non-verbal cues (body language), to indicate that you are now no longer interested in talking. Turning away slightly and/or looking off into the distance often helps get the message across. If this does not work, try saying something like:

'I should go and catch up with Fred now – there are a couple of things we need to discuss.'

or

'Time is marching on – I'd better go and get the shopping done.'

4. Assertively dealing with a nagger using the 'Fog' technique

This is an effective technique for dealing with someone who nags you, or who tries to force their views on you. The Fog technique involves communicating to them that they *may* be right, or that they *could* be right. You 'cloud' or 'fog' the issue by not actually telling them they *are* right.

Here is how you can use the Fog technique:

Jack	*'Lyn tells me you are getting a painter in to go over the house. You know, now that you are retired you should do this yourself – you will save a fortune!'*
Brian	*'Yes, it would save money but quite frankly I hate painting and I can afford to pay for it.'*
Jack	*'Yes but now that you have the time you would probably find that you would enjoy the challenge.'*
Brian	*'You may be right.' (Fog)*
Jack	*'Of course I am right! You could go on a trip with the money you save.'*
Brian	*'Hmm! Well, you could be right.' (Fog)*

In most cases, using the Fog technique will eventually cause the nagger to run out of steam. However, if they persist in annoying you, try the following:

Jack	*'What's all this "you may be right" stuff – why don't you just admit that I am right?'*
Brian	*'I don't agree with you. Let's change the subject.'*

Again, the two goals here are to assert your right not to agree, and to maintain the self-esteem and friendship of your partner or friend.

5. Assertively achieving your rights in business dealings

While modern consumer laws and competitive business practices now provide *some* consumer protection from the old 'let the buyer beware' attitudes of years ago, poor customer service remains a problem. Some business people will resist meeting their obligations by trying to fob you off when you request what is rightfully yours. Consequently, you can find that rectifying unsatisfactory service takes resolve and determination to achieve.

The key is to say to yourself, 'I am not asking for anything unreasonable here – it is my right to get the goods and services that I pay for.' Once you have this position firmly fixed in your mind, it becomes much easier to approach the shop assistant or business person and to simply and calmly request a satisfactory outcome.

Customer	*'I'd like to return this shirt – the stitching around the collar is faulty.'*
Retailer	*'Let's see! Oh dear, I can hardly see it. Nobody will notice that, it's just a very small imperfection.'*

Customer	*'Yes, it is small but it is an imperfection and I would like to exchange it, please.'*
Retailer	*'Well, I'm afraid that was the last one - we will be getting another delivery in about eight weeks - give me your phone number and I'll call you then.'*
Customer	*'I bought the shirt to wear now. If you can't replace it now I would like my money back.'*
Retailer	*'We don't usually refund money on returned articles.'*
Customer (ignoring this ploy)	*'Fine - here is my credit card for the refund.'*

The customer remains polite and reasonable while assertively requesting their rights. There is simply no need to become heated, angry or upset.

Just as important here is the use of the non-verbal behaviour (body language), that we discussed earlier in this chapter. It is the combination of direct and honest verbal behaviour, and non-verbal assertive behaviour, that provides the full power of assertive behaviour.

6. Assertively defusing a person's anger

Unfortunately, some relationships are abusive. If you believe you are in danger, or have been attacked by the person before, you need to seek help from an appropriate source. Depending on the type or severity of the problem, this assistance could range from one or both parties attending counselling to police action.

If you are not sure who to turn to, there are a number of agencies that can provide assistance that is usually free of charge. For example, telephone-based crisis referral agencies such as Lifeline can point you in the right direction.

In the meantime, defusing anger is important if violence is to be avoided. The following example shows how an assertive person may diffuse anger.

Warning: If you are in any physical danger, or if you are in a situation where alcohol or drugs are playing a role in the anger, it is wiser not to push for your rights until the situation is safe. Withdrawal from the area or the person is usually the best advice.

George (yelling)	*'You idiot – why can't you learn to control your spending? We are retired now, you know!'*
Mary	*'You are obviously very angry. Let's sit down and talk about it.'*
George	*'Talking is not going to help. You've run up a large bill on our credit card. When will you stop wasting our money?'*
Mary	*'I'd like to discuss this with you but it is really difficult when you keep yelling at me.'*
George	*'I want this spending to cease right now – we can't afford to get into debt. We'll lose the house, everything!'*
Mary	*'Then let's sit down and talk about it.'*
George	*'Okay, okay – so why did you run up the debt on our credit card last week?'*

By remaining calm and demonstrating that she wanted to resolve the issue, Mary has assertively managed George's anger down to a manageable level from which she can begin an orderly discussion.

7. Assertively using the 'broken record' technique where you are being pressured to agree to something against your will

Have you ever experienced the pressure of a well-meaning but insistent friend or relative who wants to you do something, or to go somewhere, that does not interest you? Sometimes it can be tempting to just give in and go along with them. However, there are times when we simply do not want to take part in somebody else's plans.

Here is how you use the 'broken record' technique to assert your right not to agree:

Paul	*'Damien, I've just bought a new boat. I'm taking you out fishing tomorrow afternoon.'*
Damien	*'Thanks for the offer, Paul, but I don't feel all that comfortable in boats.'*
Paul	*'Oh you don't have to worry – it's a safe boat and I am an experienced sailor.'*
Damien	*'Paul, I have no doubts about your expertise nor about the safety of your boat – I just don't enjoy being in them.'*
Paul	*'That's because you have probably been out in smaller boats with inexperienced people – I promise you that everything will be okay.'*
Damien (using the broken record technique)	*'As I say, I have no doubts about your expertise nor the safety of your boat – I just don't enjoy being in them. I'll catch up with you over the weekend for a beer.'*

In the above example, Damien would keep applying the broken record technique until Paul finally got the message. By 'softening' the process with the suggestion of catching up later for a beer, Damien achieves the joint goals of asserting his rights and maintaining Paul's self-esteem and friendship.

The broken record technique can also be used where you wish to get rid of high-pressure salespeople who are invading your privacy, or wasting your time. Of course, here you could just (aggressively) hang up the telephone, or shut the door in their face, but most people do not feel comfortable doing this. The broken record technique allows you assertively to manage the situation. Here is an example:

Telephone sales person	*'. . . and once you have used our lawn fertiliser your grass will always be greener.'*
Customer	*'I'm not interested, thank you.'*
Telephone sales person	*'If you buy our product I'll throw in an introductory 15 per cent discount. You will never go back to any other product.'*
Customer	*'No thanks, I am not interested.'*
Telephone sales person	*'Your next-door neighbour uses our products and he swears by them.'*
Customer (using the broken record technique)	*'No thanks, I am not interested.'*

In these circumstances there are no relationship issues to preserve or nurture, so you can just keep repeating 'No thanks, I am not interested' until the message sinks in. If the salesperson does not get the message after your repeated responses, you can say, 'No thanks – I am going to hang up now' then just hang up.

SUMMARY:
In this chapter we . . .

- Examined the differences between aggressive, non-assertive, and assertive behaviours.
- Listed five relationship issues requiring assertive behaviour in retirement.
- Described how to use rehearsal to develop your assertiveness skills.
- Examined ways of using assertiveness skills in relationships so that you obtain your rights while preserving the relationship.

CHECKLIST

- ☐ I understand the differences between aggressive behaviour, non-assertive behaviour, and assertive behaviour.
- ☐ I will rehearse assertive behaviour to improve my levels of assertiveness.
- ☐ I am familiar with the assertiveness techniques described in this chapter.

CHAPTER FOUR

Resolving conflict and negotiating good deals

AIMS OF THIS CHAPTER

- To understand why conflict resolution and negotiation skills are important in retirement.
- To identify what goes wrong when conflict resolution and negotiation fails.
- To provide guidelines for use during conflict or negotiation.

Why are conflict resolution skills and negotiation skills important in retirement?

Why would anyone need to be concerned about conflict management or negotiation in retirement? Surely this is a time for relaxing, having fun, and doing your own thing! On the other hand, could it be that late Australian prime minister Malcolm Fraser's now famous words 'Life was not meant to be easy' still apply even in retirement?

Effective conflict resolution and negotiation skills are helpful in the following three areas of life:

1. Relations with your partner/spouse

There have been numerous studies pointing to an increased rate of marital separation in the years immediately following retirement. This situation arises because partners can find that they have each other's undivided attention for the first time in many years. Conflict resolution skills can be helpful at this time so that partners can work through any relationship problems that surface due to the special stresses affecting them as they adjust to their new lifestyle. If teething problems are addressed early, they can then be stopped from developing into major difficulties.

2. Friends and neighbours

The lifestyles of friends and neighbours, which were barely noticed when you were at work during the day, may now escalate into a range of annoying, intrusive behaviours. These annoyances will require careful resolution if neighbourly relationships are to remain intact and everyone is to stay calm.

3. Business dealings

For most people, retirement represents a time when financial status shifts from the wealth-accumulation phase to the wealth-preservation phase. Consequently, negotiation skills are important when it comes time to buy a new home, purchase a car, or any of the other necessities of life.

Roles, responsibilities and territorial disputes

'... and,' she said with a note of concern in her voice, 'After he retires next Friday, he is going to be here ... all the time!'

Retirement can trigger special pressures where marriage relationships have comprised older-style 'traditional' husband and wife roles where the husband is the principal breadwinner. In such relationships, wives of recently retired men frequently complain that they find their former roles and responsibilities are now devalued by a well-meaning but bored and interfering husband. For example, the weekly shopping has been known to become a battleground with arguments in the supermarket as the newly retired partner removes items from the trolley in exchange for a 'cheaper' brand.

Arguments

'Since my husband retired it seems that we have done nothing but argue and bicker, sometimes over the silliest things. It drives us both nuts but we keep going round and round in circles without resolving anything.'

The subject of ongoing arguments between partners was raised frequently by those on the *Retire 200* program. The most common causes of disputes, where both partners were retired, concerned:

- The use of leisure time.
- Finances – how much to spend and what to spend it on.
- The need of one partner to have time and space to themselves.
- Whether to move from the family home or not.
- Accepting responsibility for maintenance, cleaning, and other essential duties around the home.

As we look at the various styles of decision-making it is important to understand that the style we use when trying to win arguments is often drawn from the styles we saw our parents use when they were arguing. Consequently, our expectation of what is effective and what is not may be based on the style of the parent we saw winning most of the arguments. For example, was the 'winner':

- Quiet, measured and reasonable?
- Yelling, crying and screaming?
- Using clever linguistic ability and logic to win arguments?
- The loudest parent?

Ineffective (but commonly used) styles of resolving conflict

Let us now look at the four most commonly occurring but ineffective styles that we may adopt when attempting to resolve conflict:

Style 1: Aggressors

Aggressors are typified by the following behaviours:

- Winning is the only acceptable outcome – there are few rules, and strategies may include physical or psychological violence.
- Screaming, yelling, and threatening may be part of the process.
- Cold logic is applied even if this clearly ignores the emotional needs of the other person.

- It is not important if the vanquished is happy about the outcome or not . . .

When arguments are won in this way, the aggressive winner may feel good for a short time. However, such victories are not really 'won' in the long term. Eventually the loser may start applying 'passive' aggression such as moping about or showing their resentment and anger in other ways. Consequently, if the vanquished is unhappy in the relationship life will soon become miserable for the aggressor too. In other words, the aggressor might win the battle using this method, but they will not win the war!

Style 2: Peacemakers

Peacemakers are typified by the following behaviours:

- They fear situations where discussions appear to be about to escalate into an argument.
- They have a high need to keep interactions polite and unheated.
- They give in to satisfy others' demands to calm things down and maintain the peace.

Peacemakers feel better in the short term because the perceived unpleasantness has dissipated. However, it will eventually occur to them that they have sacrificed what is rightfully theirs. They may then soon resent the fact that their partner does not really have their interests at heart. Like those who lose to the 'Aggressors', they may resort to passive aggression by regularly harping about their good-natured preparedness to back down. Their aim is to make the winner feel guilty but nobody really wins in the long term.

Style 3: Avoiders

Avoiders are typified by the following behaviours:

- They avoid conflict at all costs.
- They will change the subject to avoid confrontation.

- They try to distract the other person by introducing a 'safer' topic to try to get them off contentious subjects.
- They will even physically leave the room to avoid conflict.

Avoiders find that their anxiety diminishes in the short term. However, any ongoing problems between the Avoider and the other person remain unresolved. Consequently, the problem continues to bubble under the surface and will re-emerge to disrupt the relationship at some other time.

For those living around Avoiders, the situation can be equally as frustrating. Issues that are annoying them, and which they would prefer to discuss, or bring to a head, continue to impact on the relationship. Again, there are no winners when this style of problem-solving is used.

Style 4: Givers and takers

Givers and takers have one major behaviour:

- They compromise on the understanding that the other party compromises too.

To a casual observer, the process used by givers and takers appears to be fair and reasonable. However, in reality nobody wins and nobody loses. Everyone acts and feels terribly civilised, but both parties go away frustrated in their attempt to resolve the problem. Consequently, the problem blows up again the next time the issue arises.

Developing conflict resolution and negotiation skills

Conflict resolution skills and negotiation skills share a number of steps and processes. Both sets of skills involve applying a range of interpersonal processes so that mutually agreeable outcomes result. The key difference between the two is that in the case of negotiation skills the event is usually yet to occur – for example, selling a house or buying a car. In conflict resolution, the event or the decision has usually already occurred, with negative consequences for one or both parties – for example, a dispute between neighbours over the disturbance caused by a barking dog.

Another significant difference between the two processes can relate to the level of the interpersonal relationships involved.

In negotiation, the relationship is:

- either nonexistent (for example, purchasing a house from a stranger), or,
- at least functional (for example, negotiating with members of the extended family regarding who is going to use a shared holiday house at Easter).

Conflict resolution, however, involves arriving at agreement on a subject that has already become highly emotionally charged and where the relationship of the parties involved is either ailing or has broken down altogether.

Improving conflict resolution skills

It can be helpful to view conflict as the natural outcome that results from the differing views and opinions that people hold. In most cases, society's diverse opinions and attitudes enrich our environment by promoting variety. As an example, if you sent twelve people into a shop and instructed them to buy a 'tasteful' outfit, the range of outfits purchased would be diverse. Unfortunately, the very same diversity that promotes cultural and artistic richness also extends to opinions regarding the correct height of neighbours' fences, the acceptable frequency of a dog's bark, and the levels of noise from late-night parties next door.

In Australia and New Zealand there is a growth industry dedicated to providing professional services in the area of conflict resolution. Since the early 1990s, a number of municipalities have offered conflict resolution services to assist in the resolution of disputes among neighbours. There are also a number of legal firms offering similar dispute resolution services for issues arising between businesses and their clients.

Of course, there is little doubt that when it comes to managing conflict, prevention is better than cure. However, as conflict is inevitable where people with differing interests and values interact, it is important that we are all able to manage conflict. If we can also view conflict as an opportunity for growth then so much the better!

The win–win concept

Modern conflict resolution involves applying what has become known as the 'win–win' concept. This process has proven to be so successful that the term 'win–win' has now entered everyday language and is used to describe practically any interaction between people where nobody is disadvantaged.

Win–win works on the premise that if people involved in a dispute discuss their needs collectively, and work together to find a solution that meets their individual 'interests', it is possible to reach a conclusion where everyone's needs are met. In other words, nobody loses – hence, win–win.

An example of win–win at a very basic level could involve the following example of the shift worker who needs to sleep during the day when the retiree next door chooses to play loud music. One person needs to sleep; one person is exercising their right to play music during the day. Here is the example of conflict resolution using the compromise model, followed by an example using the win–win process.

Compromise model:

Retiree: asked to compromise by turning down the volume	*'But if I turn down my amplifier I can't hear the rhythm section clearly; and anyway rock is meant to be loud – it's not background music!'*
Shift worker: asked to sleep in a room on the other side of the house during the day	*'My wife and children use the other rooms and my sleeping on that side of the house would inconvenience them – working night shift is bad enough as it is!'*

Win-win model

Retiree and shift worker meet to discuss their needs and interests, and a practical win–win solution is found	*Retiree: 'When I am playing CDs I will close the two windows on your side of my house as well as the connecting door from the lounge room to the room nearest your side of the house.'* *Shift worker: '. . . and I'll shut my bedroom window.'*

Meeting 'interests' rather than 'positions'

When people are in conflict they invariably come up with their own 'position' quite early in the process.

One neighbour might say:

'I must have a high fence for privacy.'

The other neighbour might say:

'I can't tolerate high fences – they make me feel like I'm in a prison.'

Once these opinions are aired they can be difficult to back away from gracefully. Conflict resolution experts refer to such rigidity of thinking as 'arguing from a position'. On the other hand, when the win–win process is applied the parties in the dispute are encouraged to identify their real needs. In win–win parlance, these needs are called 'interests'.

Interests include our concerns, wants and needs, and are usually the real reason for the dispute in the first place. For example, when one neighbour takes the position 'I must have a high fence', their real 'interest' might be 'I want privacy'. Likewise when the other neighbour takes the position, 'I could not bear a high fence', their real interest may be, 'I want natural light in my kitchen and hobbies room'. Therefore, when we negotiate with the aim of meeting everyone's interests, we open up a range of possible options from which we can select one that works for all parties.

Here are some compelling reasons for concentrating on interests rather than on positions.

The cycle of bickering

When people argue regularly, particularly within a close relationship, they sometimes fall into the habit of never genuinely attempting to resolve the dispute. It may be that the argument started out over who should take out the rubbish or who should vacuum the house. Unfortunately, over time the argument may deteriorate into a contest to see who gives in first. On the other hand, if the discussion centres on each other's interests, and both people start looking for a win–win, the pressure to keep fighting dissipates.

In the above situation, the real issue or 'interest' may concern the equitable division of labour around the house now that both partners have retired from the workforce. Arguing from positions may mean the husband says, 'But my wife has always done the vacuuming – why should I start doing it now?' His wife may be saying, 'But that was when you were working full time and I was only working two days a week. It's your turn now!'

If the partners were to focus on interests – in this case, the equitable division of labour – then they could generate a list of the important jobs that need doing around the house and agree to split them up fairly. It may then turn out that the husband takes over the vacuuming while his wife washes the car, or that she continues to vacuum while he takes on other responsibilities such as hanging out the washing.

Permanency

Another dilemma, common in relationship disputes, occurs when the same old argument repeatedly resurfaces. This situation invariably occurs when people are arguing from positions and the only way to end the argument is for one person to lose, or for both to compromise. The result is that no one is truly satisfied and the real problem-solving process ends up being perpetually postponed.

An example of the above situation could be where one partner likes to watch the football on television on Saturday afternoons yet finds that his wife dislikes the raucous background noise of the sporting commentators. If a compromise solution was used – such as turning the volume down low – neither party would really be satisfied. The football fan would be straining to hear the match details and might feel that the atmosphere of the game was being lost. His wife would still be annoyed to hear the irritating commentary, albeit at a lower volume.

On the other hand, by discussing their respective interests a mutually satisfying solution could be found. For example, the husband could buy a set of high-quality lightweight headphones with which to listen to the match. The needs and interests of both parties would then be met.

Versatility

Another reason for focusing on interests is the sheer range of potential options that become available when solutions are examined collaboratively. When people begin to work as a team they enhance their ability to think creatively and to generate options for meeting everyone's interests. Clearly, the more potential options that become available, the greater the likelihood of finding a solution that is aligned to the interests of all parties.

Suggested guidelines for conflict resolution

In my own dealings with clients, I have found the following points to be helpful. They are an amalgam of the procedures used by modern practitioners of conflict resolution.

Setting the right environment for discussion

Before arranging the meeting with the others involved in the dispute, give some thought to how and where you will hold the meeting. Importantly, the venue needs to be on neutral territory so that no one feels at an advantage or disadvantage. A very natural reaction when we are under stress is to want to physically escape from the situation. This reaction is known as the 'flight or fight' reaction and is powerfully installed in the primitive limbic system of our brain. Consequently, it is not wise to hold the meeting in a small stuffy room where people may feel hemmed in during stressful moments.

Creating the right physical environment is only one part of the equation. It is also important that the right psychological and social environment is created. Therefore, while you may not be feeling terribly charitable towards the people involved in the dispute, try to go out of your way to put them at ease and to make them feel safe. Encourage them to feel that the process will be worth their while. Before getting into the main discussion, tell them you are confident that by working together you and they will come up with some ideas that will be mutually acceptable.

Clarify everyone's perceptions of what the conflict is really about

It is important that you take all the time necessary to establish what the core issues of conflict are. Remember not to confuse the *person* with the *problem*. For example, it is not your *neighbour* who is causing you stress but the idea that a high fence may *block out the natural light* to your kitchen.

It is also a good idea to discuss who is going to have their say first. Have everyone agree that once someone is having their turn to talk, they should be allowed to speak uninterrupted. This process allows everyone to get their issues out into the open and to feel that they have been heard. It can also break new ground by allowing people to hear each other's perceptions of the problem – possibly for the first time.

When deciding who is to start the discussion, offer the other person the opportunity to speak first. In some instances, particularly where trust between the parties is very low, the other person may wish you to go first for fear that you may capitalise on their disclosure. If you sense this is their concern, by all means go first.

Use language carefully

Be careful about how you structure your language so that you do not inadvertently sound as if you are in 'blaming' mode. For example, instead of saying 'You are making my life miserable', say, 'It will be difficult for me if I have to work in artificial light in my kitchen.'

Ask questions to ensure that you are clear about how the other person perceives the problem. Then, listen carefully to what everyone says and provide feedback to them that demonstrates you are hearing and understanding the content of their message (see the chapter on Communication for more information about attending skills). As you listen, try to empathise with their position; reassess whether *you* are being completely honest and reasonable. Where you find that you have entered the discussion with an erroneous perception of the situation, be honest and disclose this to them.

Encourage collaborative effort

Try to encourage a team approach to solving the dispute. The conflict will not be resolved until all parties genuinely and completely support proposed solutions. It can be very easy at this time for one or more people in the dispute to dominate by using their strength of personality against a less powerful person. If the discussions then conclude on apparent agreement which is really due to dominance at the discussion table, the 'agreement' will be short lived and will collapse once all parties are back on their own territories. Lasting decisions only occur where everyone's interests are considered and where a process of collaborating to generate options for moving forward is genuinely agreed.

Look forward instead of dwelling on the past

Like most of the components of conflict resolution, looking forward demands a certain degree of generosity from all parties. Dwelling on past events, skirmishes, or insults will not help move the process towards an effective outcome. Therefore agree to try to focus on the problem as it is now. Resist the temptation to drag up the details of old disagreements, particularly when they focus on some of the less attractive aspects of human nature.

A further goal of effective conflict resolution should be to not only address the issues but to try to restore the relationships between those who may now not be on comfortable speaking terms. Once the relationship has been re-established, any further issues that arise can be more easily resolved without escalating into yet another dispute.

Develop a range of possible options

As options are being generated, keep an open mind and try not to be too quick to discount the ideas of others. When generating options, ask for the other person's contributions first and acknowledge the positive aspects of their suggestions. Suggest using a 'brainstorming' approach, that is, have a session where ideas and options are generated to meet the interests of everyone, and critical discussion or rejection of ideas is postponed until the list is complete.

When going through the list of options generated, encourage each other to look for common threads and then work together on the options that seem most likely to satisfy everyone's needs.

Generate a list of agreed actions

This is one of the most important stages in the conflict resolution process. It is when everyone starts to agree on some small steps that they can move forward with before resolving the main issue.

For example, if you and your partner are dealing with a wide range of issues that are affecting your happiness, the 'one small step at a time' strategy is a wise idea. Trying to radically change the complex dynamics of a relationship overnight is unlikely to work and will just serve to diminish everyone's belief that change is possible.

Write an agreement that summarises the benefits

Once there is agreement from all parties concerning the way forward, it is important to draw up a written list of the agreed actions or decisions. Next to this list write a brief description of the benefits to each person concerned in the dispute.

Note: Where actions such as building a fence are involved, it is important to ensure that completion dates are built into the agreement so that the 'solution' is not avoided by one party.

EXAMPLE OF AN ACTION STATEMENT

ACTION STATEMENT	**BENEFITS**
1. We have agreed to build a wooden fence 175 cm high. 2. We will obtain at least three quotes from reputable fencing contractors. 3. We will meet by 15 March to decide which contractor will get the work. 4. The construction of the fence is to be commenced by 30 April.	**For Julie**: Natural light will continue to reach the kitchen and hobbies room. **For Peter**: A 175 cm fence will provide privacy and will stop my young children from gaining access to the busy road through Julie's property.

Julie Street ....

Peter Jones ....

Once the agreement is drawn up and signed, everyone should be given a copy to retain. If memories about what was agreed blur later, the Action Statement provides the evidence required.

Dealing with emotions during conflict resolution

The above methods for resolving conflict have long been applied successfully by professionals in the area of conflict resolution. However, for those who have never engaged in conflict resolution before, the prospect can feel quite threatening. This is particularly true when the conflict has been drawn out over time, and where those involved have allowed the situation to deteriorate to the level of personal accusations and insults. Under these circumstances, it is understandable when people become apprehensive about their ability to deal with emotions such as anger and resentment – either their own or those of others.

In this next section we will look at ways in which you can handle your own emotions and those of others during the dispute resolution process.

Focus on the problem

'Leaving your ego at the door' is highly recommended when you are entering into dispute resolution. If we allow our egos and feelings to take over, we will soon find out that they interfere with the real goal of the exercise, which is to focus on solving the problem.

The following ego-based emotional reactions are among those that most often block effective conflict resolution.

(a) *Reacting defensively*: for example, interpreting comments expressed about the problem as a personal attack.
(b) *Point scoring*: for example, throwing in 'cheap shots' that are of a personal nature but which have little to do with solving the actual problem.

(c) *Accusing*: for example, implying that the problem is mainly the fault of the other person.
(d) *Going on the attack*: for example, attempting to undermine the confidence of others by a personal attack such as, 'If you had not (done such and such), everything would be okay.'

Handling outbursts of anger from the other party

When people are angry or hurt, they may resort to a personal verbal attack. It is very easy, especially during the heat of the moment, to take these comments personally and to respond in kind. However, self-indulgent responses of this type usually signal the end to any meaningful discussion, at least until everyone has had time to calm down again. Unfortunately, in the meantime more ruminating and brooding will usually have occurred and gaining a successful resolution to the problem becomes even more difficult to achieve.

If you find that the other party is becoming angry, there are a number of steps that you can take to help defuse their anger. Understand, however, that applying these steps takes a hefty degree of emotional maturity, generosity and self-discipline on your part.

(a) *Let them get the matter off their chest*: In counselling circles this process is known as 'venting'. It allows the other person to release some of their built-up anger and resentment. It is important during this time to resist the natural urge to interrupt. Just listen to them quietly and try to convey the impression that you are not judging them. To do this, you need to be aware of your non-verbal language: do not raise your eyebrows at their comments, don't smirk or appear smug.
(b) *Try not to react defensively*: Whether it is intended or not, people will sometimes use language that can easily be taken personally as you listen to them describe the problem. For example, instead of saying, 'I get upset when I think about the

natural light I will lose if a high fence goes up', they may say, 'The thought of you building your stupid fence is causing me a lot of stress.' It is very easy to find yourself bristling when you are on the receiving end of this type of language, but try to put their remarks in the context of the real concerns they are trying to convey and the emotions they are experiencing.

Managing your own emotions

There are a number of steps that you can take to manage your own emotions during the resolution process.

(a) *Preparation*: Make a list of your 'interests' so that they are clear and accessible when you are under pressure. Even the most eloquent speaker can become 'tongue tied' during the heat of the moment; having a list in front of you will help you to remain focused on the important points.
Make a list of the points you believe the other person will raise. The thinking behind this idea is that it helps you to see the situation as they may be seeing it. You may then find it easier to see the dispute in terms of interests rather than perpetuating the blaming stance that can result from only looking at the issues from your own position.

(b) *Rehearse relaxation techniques*: Here you can apply an abbreviated version of the diaphragmatic breathing exercises described in the chapter on anxiety, depression and stress. The following method of relaxation differs slightly from the process described in that chapter, in that it can be used if you find yourself getting heated *during* the resolution process.
   (i) Slowly take a deep breath and hold it in for a couple of seconds.
   (ii) Tell yourself to relax and then slowly breathe out again.
   (iii) Relax your muscles as you breathe. Say to yourself, 'I am relaxing and staying calm'.

(iv) Refocus your mind and energy on the process of resolving the conflict.

What to do if you become emotional

Sometimes, despite your best intentions, you may find yourself losing control of your emotions. It may be that you are mulling over something someone has said, and which you have interpreted as an insult. However, as we discussed earlier, it is not helpful to react at the same level. Remaining cool in the face of provocative behaviour will enhance your credibility in the eyes of all of those present.

Here are three steps you can take to convey the impression that you are in control, even if inwardly you feel like exploding. These methods are very powerful and are used extensively by negotiation and conflict resolution specialists.

(a) *Focus on interests*: take a deep breath and continue to focus on interests rather than on getting even with the other person.
(b) *Interpret insults as unintentional*: give the other person the benefit of the doubt even if you are privately convinced that their comments were designed to hurt or annoy you. You might have misunderstood them, but in any case putting a generous interpretation on their words will help you achieve the real goal of solving the problem.
(c) *Act as if you are relaxed*: simply acting as if you are relaxed helps you return to a more stable emotional level. On the other hand, succumbing to your feelings is likely to result in you winding yourself up even further. By staying calm in the face of the other person, you reduce the likelihood of them becoming angry too.

The following steps will help you act, and then become, calm:

- Maintain your normal volume when speaking.
- Try to keep your voice even so that any hurt or exasperation does not show.

- Remember to maintain appropriate eye contact – if you suddenly start redirecting your gaze elsewhere, or looking down while you speak, you will alert the other person to your discomfort.
- Do not fidget or wave your hands around.

Improving negotiation skills

Until now, we have discussed win–win methods of solving disputes where it is also important to rebuild or maintain a relationship. When you are negotiating with family or friends ('Let's go to a movie' versus 'Let's go out for dinner'), you can also apply the win–win techniques that were discussed in the section on conflict resolution.

There are situations, however, where the person or organisation we are dealing with is not interested in our good will or in behaving ethically. They are, rather, focused on getting our money and as much of it as possible!

In the following section we are going to examine some ways in which you can beat hard-headed, rough, tough negotiators at their own game. For the purposes of this discussion we will look at the skills you could apply to the process of buying a car.

There are two reasons for using the car example:

- Nearly everyone will need to buy a car at some time during their retirement.
- The car sales industry is a good example because the sales strategies they sometimes use are about as tough as they get.

These comments are bound to draw reactions from car salespeople such as, 'But we are not like that any more' or 'We are customer focused these days!' To be a little generous, let us acknowledge that there are good, reputable car salespeople out there. In fact, in the case of large dealerships, a large component of their future cash stream can come from providing the ongoing service and maintenance of your car; consequently, they have a strong vested interest in keeping you on side as a potential service customer. However, visit a second-hand car lot and you are still likely to find yourself in a tough negotiating environment where after-sales service ranges from low priority to non-existent.

Know your adversary

When you are negotiating with tough business people, there is much you can do to establish the balance of power in your favour. The old saying 'Knowledge is power' is particularly apt in these circumstances. Therefore, DO YOUR HOMEWORK! For example, when the car industry was researched for this section of the book, three car salespeople were consulted. The following facts were discovered about the ways in which car salespeople may operate.

1. The remuneration of car salespeople is usually a combination of salary and sales commission. Therefore, they are under great pressure to make sales. Think back to when you were working full time – how would you have reacted if the boss suddenly told you that you would only be paid if you brought in new customers to the organisation?
2. In the car sales business only the tough survive – even other car salespeople want their colleagues to fail so that more of the potential customers who walk into the car yard are *theirs*!
3. Car salespeople attend seminars, listen to audio recordings, watch video clips, and talk with other salespeople on the topic of how to get the sale. 'Getting the sale' means getting your signature on a contract and getting the money.
4. In some car sales businesses, the salesperson who sells the least number of cars for the month or quarter 'leaves' and a new salesperson takes their place.

5. Car salespeople are highly competitive and, apart from making money, are often motivated by winning the car yard's 'salesperson of the month' or other recognition-based sales competition. The winners of these competitions are not the salesperson who customers nominate for providing the best service, but the ones who sells the most cars.
6. Customers who are considerate, polite, and who do not try to drive a hard bargain are often derisively referred to as 'wood-ducks' due to their lack of aggression or strategies to 'avoid capture'.
7. Car salespeople and the concept of after-sales service are frequently at opposite ends of the continuum. Customers who return to speak to the salesperson because they are unhappy with the car they have purchased may be referred to as 'ghosts' because they come back to haunt the salesperson with problems.

What they 'know' about you

The point of the above exercise is to demonstrate that by doing some basic research, you can gain information that gives you inside knowledge, which is important as you negotiate. For example, if you think the car salesperson was simply paid a salary, you may have approached them differently than you would otherwise, understanding the financial pressure they are under to make sales. It is also important to know how they operate, because within a few minutes of you walking into a car yard, they know a lot about *you* and *your* individual buying behaviours.

For example:

1. They already know you would love to buy a new car no matter how blasé you try to appear. You would not be there if you were not at least interested in the idea of a new car.
2. They are trained to look for buying signals. For example, if you touch the car while you are discussing it, this could be

interpreted as meaning that you are starting to regard it as your own property. Other signals you give away can be verbal: 'Can you get these with cruise control?' Why would you ask that if you were not interested in the car?

3. They carefully watch your non-verbal (body) language. For example, a furtive smile of approval to your partner as the salesperson brings the price down closer to your budget.
4. Car salespeople who have been in the industry for a while pick up signals from you that even *they* would have difficulty explaining. It seems that when a customer is ready to buy, they unwittingly display an array of verbal and non-verbal buying signals that give the game away. These all indicate to the salesperson that it is time move in and make the sale.

What can *I* do to negotiate successfully?

Know the seller's competition

- Let the salesperson know that you are talking to their competitors.
- Have business cards from their nearest rival that you display during the discussion.
- Mention the competition's salesperson by name as if you already have established a close business relationship with them.
- If the car has an equivalent model in another brand, discuss it with the salesperson to let them know you are an informed buyer.

Play tough – be prepared not to buy

Before you walk onto the car lot, make a decision not to buy unless you get a certain price. By taking this step, you will have more confidence and will be able to look the salesperson in the eye while saying, 'If I can't buy it for this amount, I can't buy it.' Notice the use of the words 'can't buy it' rather than 'won't buy it'. As mentioned before, most sales people are very competitive and you need to ensure that when you negotiate with them you do not turn the exercise into a personal challenge. If you inadvertently succeed in stirring up an ego-based challenge, they may just be prepared to lose the sale to beat you at your own game.

Use time as your most powerful weapon

Salespeople use time to generate sales with such monotonous regularity that usually we are not even aware that we are falling for it. For example, special prices that 'end at midday Sunday' are a common way that time is used to pressure us into buying now or risk missing a bargain. However, you too can use time to bluff salespeople.

> *Customer: 'I have until Monday to get some money that has fallen due from an investment back into a term deposit. At the moment, the money is burning a hole in my pocket, which is why I am looking at this car. If you can get the price down to $X by Monday I'll buy it from you. If you can't, don't worry – I understand you can't work miracles. I'll just do the sensible thing and reinvest my money instead of buying this car.'*

Having delivered the above soliloquy, make an excuse to leave immediately as you hand them your telephone number 'just in case they can get the price down'. Unless they have completely given up, the salesperson will probably ring you well before Monday with a price somewhere between what you have asked for and what they have offered before. It is very important at this time that you do not speak to them personally. Have someone else take your calls before Monday to keep you away from the salesperson, or vet your calls through voicemail if you have it.

On Monday, call them mid-afternoon to get their verdict. Remember, by then they believe you have only a couple of hours before you must make your decision – the pressure on them is now enormous if they really want the sale! All of this may sound sneaky but, as we have discussed, they will not hesitate to use their own tricks of the trade on you.

Whether you are buying a car, a house, or a new outfit, the above rules apply. Do your research, know the seller's competitors, and, above all, be prepared to walk out without buying on the day.

SUMMARY:

In this chapter we . . .

- Listed situations where conflict resolution and negotiation skills may be required.
- Identified the four most ineffective styles of resolving conflict used by most people.
- Learned how to apply the 'win–win' process to resolving conflict.
- Learned how to manage emotions during conflict resolution.
- Identified why it is important to know our competitors when negotiating.
- Learned to use time as a powerful negotiating tool.

CHECKLIST
Conflict Resolution Skills

- ☐ I will avoid using the four most common ineffective styles of conflict resolution.
- ☐ I understand the win–win process and the importance of examining everyone's interests rather than their positions.
- ☐ I understand how to manage my emotional levels when discussions become heated.
- ☐ I understand how to deal with the emotional outbursts of others.

CHECKLIST
Negotiation Skills

- ☐ I understand the need to know my adversary.
- ☐ I understand how to apply the powerful tool of time and how not to let others use time to my disadvantage.
- ☐ I understand the importance of being prepared not to buy on the day.

CHAPTER FIVE

Maintaining effective relationships with your partner and friends

AIMS OF THIS CHAPTER

- To examine how shared values and interests impact on the wellbeing of relationships.
- To examine ways of building shared values and interests to maintain healthy relationships.

Why shared values are important in relationships

An excellent example of the power of shared values and interests occurs when people become stuck in a lift together at work. Regardless of their normal status in the organisation, the chairman of the board, the junior personal assistant, and the bike courier will all find themselves chatting away given sufficient time stuck in the lift. Their 'shared interest' is their present situation, and how long it will be before they are rescued. Initially the conversation may centre around when they are likely to be released. Given time, it is likely that they will begin to explore other interests such as their favourite TV program or the football teams that they follow.

Having shared values and interests is important to our social wellbeing, and to the health of our relationships with our friends and family. Over the following pages we will look at how shared values help to keep people together. We will also look at how we can ensure that we continue to build shared values and interests into our special relationship with our spouse or partner.

The values we share when we are in the workforce

Have you ever noticed how in most cases, the people you were once close to at work no longer seem relevant to you after they have left the organisation? Even if you arrange a social reunion with them a year later, you essentially find yourselves focusing on topics related to your past work together. Your common values and interests were the work itself, the sharing of challenges with peers, observing the way your organisation was performing and, of course, gossip! However, once people leave an organisation, they also leave its culture and values, and the motivation to keep in regular contact with former work colleagues typically diminishes over time.

In large organisations, managers invest heavily in promoting employee bonding through shared interests and goals. They have learnt that the company Christmas party, the footy tipping contests and residential management courses all contribute to high morale, which in turn assists to build a cohesive, happy workforce. In fact, research into organisation effectiveness repeatedly demonstrates that a workforce with shared interests will typically outperform that of a rival's where the sense of belonging to a team is low or absent.

These days, enlightened employers have extended their work-based concerns about employees' morale to include 'Employer Assisted Programs' (EAPs). A typical EAP includes free counselling for the employee and for family members where relationships are going off the rails due to work-related stress, substance abuse, or even problems at school involving their children. Apart from the moral or ethical imperatives for looking after employees, such schemes reinforce the feelings of belonging to an organisation where concern for staff is entrenched.

Now it is up to you!

Once we have retired, however, most morale-building activities are left up to one person: YOU! If you are fortunate enough to be in a caring relationship then you are off to a good start. However, as the *Retire 200* research showed, this is not always the case. It is very easy for busy working couples to go about their lives in a constant state of chaos. Trying to find a balance between working, attending to family responsibilities and leisure becomes a major challenge. As such hectic lifestyles can go on for many years, it is not surprising that couples can arrive at retirement having grown apart somewhat, and without even being aware that it has happened. Now, suddenly, they have each other's prolonged and undivided attention. What were seemingly minor issues when submerged in the business of day-to-day life may become significant problems that resurface in retirement when life's work-related distractions have disappeared.

The shared values in your personal relationships

'The kids had long grown up and left home. I worked only three days a week and had become involved in volunteer work with my club. During this time, my husband continued to work long hours. On the first Monday morning of his retirement, I looked at him sitting in the lounge room reading the paper. This feels strange, I thought. I'm not sure I like this!'

When you retire, you are thrown together overnight. Some of the interests that you once shared might have ended years ago. The struggle to pay off the mortgage is over, and the kids have grown up and left home. You may even find that over the years one of you has changed their political allegiance. Consequently, it is quite common for recently retired couples to experience a wide range of emotions as they adjust to their new lifestyle together. Even in stable, happy relationships one partner may find themselves resenting their partner's intrusion into time they previously regarded as their own.

It is therefore important to ensure there are a number of values or interests which you and your partner share in common and which help to keep your relationship meaningful. Such commonalities may be your children, your religious or political beliefs, a club or sport, shared values regarding what comprises right and wrong, and, of course, mutual admiration, respect and love.

Finding commonality

'As soon as I retired we put our plan into action. We bought a caravan and took off. It may not seem very original but it was great fun – both the planning and actually doing it! We will go again next year for sure.'

The caravan trips around Australia by the 'Grey Nomads' are the result of people striving to create interesting and shared goals together. Of course, the trip itself contains intrinsic pleasures, but it is the joint processes of planning and communicating with each other that also provide much of the pleasure.

The shared values in self-help groups

Shared values and experiences are the major reasons that self-help groups work so effectively. The Returned and Services League (RSL), is an excellent example of one of Australia's first and longest surviving self-help groups. While many RSL members may not have considered their club as a self-help group, many will tell you that the only people they can really discuss their war experiences with are others who have endured similar traumas.

Building shared values in your relationship with your partner

Do a 180-degree check

As you may be aware, a common practice of many organisations when assessing the performance of employees is to take them through what is called a 360-degree feedback. This process involves the employee gaining feedback from their manager, their peers, and their direct reports. Consequently, while an employee may honestly believe they are performing well across a range of areas, their manager, peers, and reports may have an entirely different view. It can be a painful experience to discover that others regard you as deficient in an area where you thought you were performing well.

The following table contains a '180-degree' check for use between you and your partner. It essentially contains the components of the 360-degree feedback format minus the manager's and the direct reports sections. It is designed to help you verify whether you and your partner (or friends) have similar perceptions about each other and where your areas of commonality of attitude and opinion lie.

The process works by completing the table *as you see yourself* and simultaneously having your friend or partner complete the table *as they see you.* You both repeat the process for your partner. When you have finished, compare your impressions of yourself with your partner's impression of you, and have them do the same. You can photocopy the blank questionnaire in Appendix A for extra 180-degree forms.

If you do not like what you learn from the 180-degree check, take the bad news with dignity and maturity – make a decision to try to improve. Try not to regress into childhood by yelling, screaming, pouting or denial. Instead, rejoice in your shared values and take remedial action if you find that differing values are placing a strain on the relationship.

THE 180-DEGREE CHECK

Area
My general planning ability
My money management
My consideration for my partner's feelings
My consideration for my partner's needs for autonomy and time alone
My consideration for my partner's need for joint activities with me
The degree to which I accept responsibility for duties around the home
The level of empathy I demonstrate when my partner is not well or is sad
The degree to which I am prepared to attend an outing I will dislike but which I know my partner will enjoy
The number of little things I do that say 'I love you'
The level of respect I show for my partner's wishes and opinions
The manner in which I speak to my partner at home
The manner in which I speak to my partner in public
My preparedness to be welcoming and polite to friends of my partner who I do not like
The effort I make to be pleasant when I am in a bad mood or upset
The level of responsibility I take for communicating with our children and grandchildren
My preparedness to answer the telephone when neither of us feels like it
The level to which we share driving on a long trip
My sense of humour
Other?
Other?
Other?
Other?
Other?

	Terrible, ghastly	Needs to improve	Fair to average	Quite good	A saint

Decision-making and Task-allocation (DMTA) matrix

If the above process did not cause World War III in your household, and you believe that further assessment of your relationship can improve its overall functioning, try this next exercise. It is called the Decision-making and Task-allocation Matrix.

The DMTA matrix has five cells. The idea is for you to make a list of the decisions and tasks you typically share or make with your partner. You then both separately assign each decision or task to what you believe *should be* the correct cell. Here are some areas of responsibilities to start you off – add some more of your own. There is a copy of the DMTA in the Appendices.

List of responsibilities:

1. Deciding where to go for holidays
2. Setting our weekly/monthly budget
3. What colours to paint the house
4. Whether to move house or not
5. What price and style of house to purchase
6. Who looks after the tax returns
7. Who balances our budget
8. Who looks after our savings program
9. Who manages our investments
10. Who pays the bills
11. Who decides on purchases for maintenance, e.g. repairing versus buying a new hot water system
12. Who decides whether to buy new appliances, e.g. the latest TV
13. Who vacuums the house
14. Who cleans the toilets
15. Who decides what we will do today
16. Who decides who we will invite around for dinner
17. Who decides how we will maintain our health
18. YOU ADD SOME MORE

CELL A: 100%

(These tasks/decisions are completely mine, e.g. paying the bills)

CELL B: 50% – 50%

(These tasks/decisions are discussed together and voted on, e.g. where we go for holidays)

CELL C: 75% – 25%

(These tasks/decisions are discussed together but if we do not agree my partner is the decision-maker, e.g. what colour to paint the lounge room)

CELL D: 75% – 25%

(These tasks/decisions are discussed together but if we do not agree I am the decision-maker, e.g. what brand of television set to buy)

CELL E: 100%

(These tasks/decisions are completely my partner's, e.g. who looks after our tax returns)

Once you have both completed your Decision-making and Task-allocation matrices, sit down together and discuss your areas of agreement and areas of difference. Ask yourselves the following questions:

- Are you both happy with these arrangements?
- Do they expose either of you to risk should one of you become incapacitated or die?
- Is the distribution of tasks fair given that you both are now retired?
- What would you like to do differently?
- What are you going to do about the areas in which you both agree there should be change?

SUMMARY:
In this chapter we . . .

- Identified why shared values are important to the wellbeing of relationships.
- Examined the '180-degree check' and the Decision-making and Task-allocation (DMTA) matrix as measures for assessing commonality and shared values in our relationships.

CHECKLIST

- ☐ I/we will think about, and discuss, ways of building closer relationships where this is required.
- ☐ I/we will complete the 180-degree check and discuss areas where our perceptions differ.
- ☐ I/we will complete the DMTA matrix and discuss areas where there is conflict regarding our distribution of responsibilities.

CHAPTER SIX

Contributing and belonging

AIMS OF THIS CHAPTER

- To examine why we need to continue to 'belong' to society when we are retired.
- To examine ways in which the participants on the *Retire 200* project contributed to their community.
- To examine ways in which we can become involved in the community and with others.

Why 'belonging' is important

. . . in the beginning

As you would imagine, our need to belong commenced immediately after we were born. As babies we quickly began to develop attachments with the one or two adults who, in most cases, were our parents. This instinctive two-way attachment develops further as the baby 'rewards' the parents with positive responses such as smiles, happy gestures and baby gurgles. The parents respond with smiles, picking up the baby and cuddling it, contributing baby talk of their own, and providing food. Apart from the mutual pleasures of each other's company, both babies and their parents seek each other's comfort when either is anxious or in danger.

Belonging as adults – genetic selection

There is little doubt that the first human beings, like their animal counterparts, found it necessary to group together to survive the rigours of living in a dangerous environment. Humans who did not group together were left exposed to a number of potentially fatal risks:

- Those who preferred to live as individuals or in very small groups were less able to provide sufficient food and safe shelter.
- Those who preferred to live alone ran the risk of ending up on the dinner plates of wild animals or other humans.
- Those who preferred to live in small groups lacked a wide pool of available mates and consequently reduced their opportunity to breed and to continue their genetic lines.

We can therefore be reasonably sure that the humans who survived through these primitive ages were the ones who survived due to their preference for affiliating with other humans.

Affiliating

Support and assistance

Today we continue to group together for support and assistance. We need formal structures such as governments and local councils to provide our health, policing, and other community requirements. We also need the company of others so that we can fulfil our desire to feel that we are an important part of our society and community. The strength of our need to belong is borne out by the fact that there are very few voluntary hermits in the world. People who are isolated from their community tend to either be marginalised due to psychological or psychiatric disorders, or have become isolated due to poverty, illness, or substance abuse problems such as alcoholism.

Fear reduction

After the Second World War, many psychologists were at a loss to explain how it was that apparently normal human beings could have inflicted the pain and misery that took place in the Nazi concentration camps. In an attempt to answer this disturbing question, a number of social experiments were conducted in the 1950s and 1960s. During the experiments, the behaviour of the participants was closely monitored as they were subjected to extreme levels of stress and coercion. In some cases those taking part in the experiments were told to give others severe electric shocks, during which the 'victims' screamed in apparent agony and terror. Later, it would be revealed to those inflicting the 'shocks' that the victims were professional actors and that, in fact, no electric shocks had been delivered.

One of the findings of these studies concerned the ways in which people sought to reduce their fear during the experiments. While those designated as the 'shockers' had to wait their turn, they were given the opportunity to wait *alone* in a room at the university with comfortable chairs and magazines, or to wait *together* in an uncomfortable waiting room. The higher their level of fear, the more likely it was that they chose to be together even though it meant waiting in the less comfortable room.*

As we get older, our needs for fear reduction through affiliation usually centre around fears about:

- Our health and how we will be cared for if we become ill.
- Whether our finances will be sufficient to support us comfortably into old age.
- Whether we will be lonely.

Social comparison

Most of us like to know how we are performing relative to the rest of society. Social comparison does not just relate to how well we are doing financially, or how our car compares to that of our neighbour. We also like to rate ourselves against others in terms of our intelligence and our attractiveness. When we compare favourably with those around us, we feel reassured. This explains why we feel most comfortable when we are mixing with people who are similar to us in age, educational level and financial status. On the other hand, if we find ourselves in an environment where most of our neighbours are wealthier, better educated, and appear to be participating in a more enjoyable, vibrant lifestyle, we may become disillusioned and dissatisfied with life.

---

* If you are asking yourself how such psychologically distressing experiments could be allowed, the answer is that today they would not be. Ethical committees are now in place in all Australian universities. Experiments which put the psychological wellbeing of those involved in a study at risk would simply not be allowed.

To fulfil the desire for community involvement

'You need to be involved in the community.'

'Find a way of being of value to your community – you will also find rewarding relationships.'

'Do things you are interested in and ensure you understand issues outside your own four walls.'

A number of people on the *Retire 200* program were keen to ensure that they played an active role in their community. There were two general reasons for this:

- Some people were concerned that without involvement in their community they would become cut off from the mainstream of life. For these people, 'community' sometimes referred to the community of their immediate neighbourhood or even of their local church. For others, it referred to the broader community of their municipality or region.
- Some people saw themselves as experienced human resources who could provide valuable input to maintain the 'social health' of the community. For example, some were concerned that local requirements of the aging be met, while others were more concerned about a lack of leisure activities for the youth of their community.

To fulfil the desire for power

'I was at the top of the company and we employed over 1500 people. You walk out of the door and it is a hell of a shock when you find that they can keep on going without you.'

While the quote from this former managing director highlights a common dilemma for retired senior managers, it is not too far removed from us all. No matter what level we have attained as employees, or in our own businesses, we all like to think that in some way we are indispensable. We want to believe that there are certain vital qualities that only we can bring to an enterprise. It is quite natural, therefore, to feel somewhat wounded when we learn that things are going well in the workplace without us.

Unfortunately, it is when our own self-esteem is taking a hammering that we can unwittingly take out our frustration on those closest to us. The immediate effects of diminished self-esteem may include responses ranging from anger to depression and withdrawal. Being the partner of someone in such an emotional state is far from pleasant. Often the partner on the receiving end of the recent retiree's distress is also adjusting to retirement – for them, the problem is compounded as they deal with their partner's emotional problems and their own adjustment to retirement.

To fulfil the desire for a purpose in life

'I was the principal of the local primary school. I loved my job and I loved the children. I can still hear the school bell chiming from where we live and my husband, who hated his job, can't understand why this sometimes reduces me to tears.'

We all need to be needed. If your partner is going through the 'just-retired blues' there is much you can do to help them. The simple act of encouraging them to talk about their feelings, and then listening carefully, is worth its weight in gold. When missing work develops into depression, professional assistance is recommended. We will discuss post-retirement depression and strategies for reducing it in more detail in Chapter Seven.

Ways to contribute and belong

Voluntary work

'Look for voluntary work.'

'Get out into the community and do work for others in which money does not change hands.'

'Volunteering is great – gives purpose to life – things that involve people make you feel good.'

'Have an interest – try voluntary work.'

'There is no tax on helping others.'

'Involve yourself in voluntary work – it has so much to offer and is so satisfying.'

'Keep as active as possible – do something useful for yourself and for others if possible.'

If there was one common sentiment expressed about voluntary work, it was *'I always get more out of it than I put into it.'* The range of voluntary positions that people held was diverse. Some people were involved in voluntary work such as helping with meals-on-wheels, working with their church, recording 'talking books' for the blind, working on committees, or serving in the shops of organisations such as The Brotherhood of St Laurence. For others, voluntary work included working for organisations such as Lifeline, visiting the terminally ill, arranging local town clean-ups, or helping newcomers learn English. There were also those who became involved by donating their time to arts councils or other special interest bodies.

Volunteers often spoke about their initial introduction to voluntary work. Many reported that they had volunteered to 'help out for a while' only to find themselves still involved years later. However, most agreed that it is not *who* you choose to help that is important; it is the sense of achievement from making a worthwhile contribution that provides the real rewards.

One man who regularly visits those suffering from terminal illness described how he was introduced to voluntary work.

'A friend of mine was diagnosed with cancer. He was in hospital for nearly a year before he died. I would visit him at least weekly and the experience was always the same. As I would travel in the lift to his ward, I would feel a sense of apprehension come over me. What was I going to talk about that would help him feel better? After a few visits it dawned on me that what I actually said did not really matter. It was far more important just to be there for him and to provide human contact.

As I would leave him at the end of each visit, I would feel an inner strength and peace. The paradox was that I seemed to be gaining strength and comfort from him!'

As this volunteer visited his friend, he became aware of other patients in the ward who appeared to have few if any visitors and he would often find himself speaking with them too. Some time after his friend died he decided to seek out lonely terminally ill patients and visit them on a regular basis.

Helping your adult children

'I believe you need to have a function in your family which adds to their net worth.'

The above comment highlights the importance of keeping close to your family. They need you to help out in their busy lives, and you need them and the fulfilment that can be gained from helping them. Many retirees report that being able to help their adult children either financially, or through providing services such as babysitting, is one of the major pleasures in their lives.

Joining

'When you are retired you find you have a need for an identity or a peer group to belong to.'

There are a number of groups catering for retired people. For those who wish to mix socialising with learning there are campuses of the University of the Third Age (U3A) in most parts of Australia. Some retirees attend classes at U3A, while others lecture or run courses in an area in which they possess skills. Consequently, people attending U3A, whether as students or lecturers, gain the opportunity to mix with others of similar interests while also gaining intellectual stimulation.

'You need to meet with people similar to yourself otherwise you feel isolated from society.'

PROBUS (for retired people with a professional or business background) is a very popular organisation. In many PROBUS clubs there is no requirement to have either a professional or business background. Other groups, based on membership of people with similar interests, include retired employees' associations, Rotary, and Lions clubs.

The Australian Men's Shed Association (AMSA)

The Australian Men's Shed Association (AMSA) is one of Australia's largest community development programs with a predominantly male demographic. Funded by the Federal Department of Health,

AMSA was established in 2007 with the aim to support and promote the almost 1000 Men's Sheds in Australia.

Men's Sheds are non-profit community-based groups that wish to improve health and wellbeing of members and to reduce the number of men at risk from preventable health issues, particularly when those issues are exacerbated by isolation, by providing safe and friendly environments in which men can work on meaningful projects.

At the Men's Shed in Paynesville, Victoria, numerous projects keep the men busy. None of their work is for personal gain, with recent projects at Paynesville ranging from repairing furniture for people in the community to making new doors for the local Masonic Lodge.

No one feels the need to work if they do not wish to or are unable to due to poor health – some men come along simply to enjoy the camaraderie gained from associating with other men. This environment is consistent with the central aims of the sheds, which are to promote men's health and to provide men with a purpose in life while preventing social isolation and depression. Those with specialised skills find that they enjoy using them to benefit the community and, in some cases, to impart their knowledge and skills to other men at the shed.

At the Paynesville men's shed a bell is rung at ten o'clock each morning and the men must then stop working on their projects and move to the kitchen/social area. Here they sit around in a group and chat over a cup of tea or coffee. The morning tea break may go on for three quarters of an hour as the men become engrossed in their conversations.

'One of the men cooks scones which he brings in for our morning tea break. We sit around enjoying scones, jam and cream while we socialise.'

The charter of the Men's Shed dictates that three sessions a year must be run in an area pertinent to men's health.

'At a recent session on hearing loss, deficits were found in my own level of hearing and I now have hearing aids.'

Their website mensshed.org has a 'shed finder' which will point you to your nearest Men's Shed. In New Zealand, the website is menzshed.org.nz

Women's clubs and associations

'Women should take up a hobby in their 50s and join/form a group of women they see outside work. If you have that group and then lose your husband or your job, they are still there for you.'

It would be going out on a controversial limb to state that women are more supportive of each other than are men. However, during interactions with the participants on the *Retire 200* research it was common to encounter women who were members of women's groups who had been together for many years and who continued to offer each other company and support. One particular group of women comprised fifteen teachers and ex-teachers who met for lunch on a monthly basis. They gave and received emotional support from each other at these meetings and intended to maintain the group for the rest of their lives.

Successful women's groups – why they work

The successful women's groups generally have two key elements in common:

- The women had some form of shared interest. Interests ranged from membership of the same previous occupation to sharing an interest in oil painting or a craft. In rural areas of Australia, commonality was sometimes as basic as the remoteness of the region in which they lived.

- In each group there were invariably one or two women whose commitment and organisational abilities ensured that the group met regularly, that birthday lists were maintained, and that meeting venues were booked.

The members of such groups typically felt that membership of a women's group was so worthwhile that women who could not find a group to join that interested them should give some thought to establishing one of their own.

Meetup

Meetup is a social networking facility that helps people meet groups of those who share common interests. There are hundreds of Meetup groups around the world and in Australia. If you go to www.meetup.com you can find a list of the groups available in your area. In the meantime, here is just a very small sample of the many groups around:

- Happy hikers
- Single parents
- Women's fun and friendship groups
- Meditation classes
- Motorcycle newbies and seasoned riders
- Beyond 30
- Badminton
- Indoor rock climbers.

'I am involved in a Meetup group for women called "Beyond 30". The women meet every Wednesday at a local cafe for coffee and a chat. For some people this is the major social event of their week. There is no commitment required to turn up and no set agenda. For many, the group can be a starting point for meeting others and from there some may become friends and meet elsewhere as their friendship develops.'

If there are no existing groups that grab your attention, you can always start your own. The website mentioned above will show you how to do this.

Social Media

Social media such as Facebook can be a valuable resource for retired people. These days, most people will have at least heard of such media or are already using it. If you need help in joining up with Facebook or the like, just ask your friends or relatives for help. Your children or grandchildren will almost certainly know what to do – failing that, have a chat to your local librarian about getting set up.

For those of you who are unfamiliar with the uses of social media, here are a few ideas:

- You can search out other Facebook members who are living almost anywhere in the world – this can be handy if you are trying to track down a long-lost school friend.
- You can join up with a range of interest forums, e.g., Caravan Clubs, Jazz Appreciation Groups, Vintage Car Clubs . . . the list is endless.

Getting involved – it takes effort!

'You need the willingness to go out and meet people – to socialise.'

Sometimes, when you are lonely or feeling down, the last thing you feel like doing is making the effort to move into a new environment and start socialising. This can be particularly difficult for those who have lost their partner and who are venturing out by themselves at a time when they feel especially vulnerable. If you have lost your partner, groups such as Solace (a self-help group for those whose partner has died) can be a safe starting place where everyone else in the room is in the same situation.

SUMMARY:

In this chapter we . . .

- Examined the factors that condition us to 'belong' in society.
- Listed the benefits the *Retire 200* participants found for affiliating with others in retirement.
- Described ways of contributing and belonging in society.

CHECKLIST

- ☐ I understand the motivators for affiliation.
- ☐ I have read the feedback from the participants on the *Retire 200* program.
- ☐ I will consider my own need to take part in community work or to join a service organisation.

SECTION THREE

Maintaining your psychological fitness

For some people, retirement signals the culmination of years of careful planning and financial preparation. The details of an extended trip have been finalised and their life's savings have been distributed across a range of investments designed to maximise income for life. The good life is about to begin!

For others, retirement has been forced by either illness, retrenchment or business closure at an age when gaining further full-time employment is less likely. In these cases, financial plans might not have been completed and retirement may be approached with nagging concerns about how long the money will last.

However, despite our plans, transitions from one stage of life to another are rarely without their surprises. Moving from secondary school to university brings its special stresses, as does the transition from life as a university student to a member of the workforce. Our transition after many years of work also brings its challenges. Some of these challenges will have been predicted by us and will cause little or no problems. Other aspects of the transition, however, will find us temporarily unsettled as we discover that some aspects of life in retirement are not quite what we had expected.

The next four chapters of the book provide a number of strategies for dealing with the range of emotional issues we may encounter during our adjustment.

CHAPTER SEVEN

Managing anxiety, depression and stress

AIMS OF THIS CHAPTER

- To understand why the process of adjusting to retirement can be associated with emotional difficulties such as anxiety, depression and stress.
- To understand the fundamental differences between anxiety, depression and stress so that we can recognise them should they occur.
- To develop a number of strategies for improving emotional wellbeing.

What can cause people to become anxious, depressed or stressed about life in retirement?

On the *Retire 200* program, the degree to which a participant was regarded as 'well adjusted' to retirement was determined by assessing their levels of retirement-related stress, anxiety and depression. Where high levels of anxiety, depression or stress were retirement related, *Retire 200* participants were regarded as less well adjusted to retirement than those whose emotional states were within a normal range.

The details of retirement-related factors influencing emotional adjustment to retirement were discussed in detail in the introduction to this book. Here is a summary of those factors:

1. Reason for retirement

Those whose retirement was forced due to retrenchment or ill health (their own or that of a relative) were more likely to be anxious, depressed and stressed than those who had retired voluntarily.

2. Age at retirement

Those who retired at age fifty-five or younger were associated with lower levels of anxiety than those who retired older.

3. Financial independence

Those who were financially independent had lower levels of anxiety, depression and stress when compared with those who were reliant on government pensions.

4. Having a Purposeful Activity

Those who engaged in Purposeful Activities of more than five hours per week were significantly less depressed and stressed in retirement than those who were inactive.

Note: A Purposeful Activity was defined as one which results in the production of something, for example, a piece of woodwork, or which provides a service to others, such as performing voluntary work for a charity. Part-time jobs were also included as Purposeful Activities (for more information see Chapter One).

5. Availability of emotional support

Those who could access emotional support from a family member or friend, if required, were less stressed than those without access to such a resource.

6. Self-promoted health activities

Self-promoted health activities were activities that people initiated to maintain their health. Activities were divided into three categories:

- Engaging in daily exercise.
- Maintaining a healthy diet.
- Having an annual medical check-up.

The findings were:

- Those participants who exercised experienced lower levels of stress.
- Those who attended to their diet were associated with lower levels of depression.
- Those who attended to all three categories were less depressed than those who attended to just one or two.

7. Planning for retirement

Those who planned for their retirement, either financially or for lifestyle reasons such as planning to travel or to be active, were less anxious, depressed or stressed than those who did not plan.

8. Receiving advice about retirement matters

Those who had sought advice before or during retirement were less depressed than those who did not seek advice.

I do not feel depressed, anxious or stressed, yet I only match up on a few of the above eight areas

Because we each have our own ways of coping, our own levels of self-esteem, and our unique ways of responding to life's events, not all of us will react in the same way to a particular set of circumstances. For example, the *overall* levels of anxiety in those participants on the *Retire 200* without a Purposeful Activity were higher than for those who were involved in an activity. However, there also would have been people who would have scored low on anxiety even though they had *no* Purposeful Activity. Similarly, while many people on very low fixed incomes found this situation depressing and stressful, some were able to successfully manage on their income.

Understanding emotional health

Given the significant impact of emotional health on our satisfaction with life in retirement, it is important to be equipped with methods for managing anxiety, depression and stress should these ever become a problem. However, before we look at some ideas for dealing with such emotional problems, it is helpful to have a basic understanding of how anxiety, depression and stress differ.

Anxiety

You will often hear the terms *anxiety*, *fear* and *phobia* used interchangeably as if they were the one concept. While they are related, they impact on people differently and can be triggered by quite different circumstances.

Anxiety (sometimes called 'free-floating anxiety')

When people are suffering from anxiety they typically describe feeling:

- constantly on edge or on the alert;
- that all is not well;
- that something bad is about to happen.

Because of the pervasive nature of anxiety-based symptoms, anxiety is often referred to as 'hypervigilance'. The psychologist Edmund Bourne has described the focus of these symptoms as being 'internal' rather than 'external'. In other words, anxiety is not usually related to a visible, external threat but is our personal response to non-specific, unrecognised danger.

At a physiological level, people who are experiencing anxiety will typically report symptoms such as:

- sweating
- dryness in the mouth
- queasiness
- rapid heartbeat.

Fear

Fear differs from anxiety in that it is usually focused on a recognisable external threat. For example, if the dog next door has bitten you it would be natural to experience fear if you later saw it running towards you as you walked down the street. Similarly, a person whose life savings are heavily exposed to a poorly performing investment may fear losing their financial independence during an unexpected downturn in the economy.

Phobias

Phobias are regular and to onlookers, often unreasonable, fears an individual may hold relating to specific circumstances or objects. For example, people suffering from agoraphobia may fear that they will panic or lose control of themselves in certain situations such as in supermarket queues, or in other crowded places. Other common phobias can include fear of lifts, fear of spiders and fear of dental procedures.

A phobia is of serious concern when:

- the symptoms are severe (for example, chest tightness, heart racing or pounding, shallow breathing, dizziness, or trembling);
- it impacts significantly on your lifestyle (for example, not going on trips to the country just in case you happen to see a spider).

The following table summarises the differences between anxiety, fear and phobias.

Anxiety	A heightened sense that something bad may happen or of being on edge. Anxiety relates to a *non-specific, unrecognised danger.*
Fear	Similar feelings to those experienced with anxiety except that the feelings relate to *recognisable, definable threats.* Examples of fear include fear of possible attack if your car breaks down in a rough area of town at night, or the fear that a recent pathology test may return a positive result.
Phobias	Phobias relate to specific places (e.g. lifts), things (e.g. spiders), or circumstances (e.g. public speaking) of which the person has learned to be afraid.

Depression

Most people suffer from some degree of depression at various times in their life.

Depression may manifest as:

- feelings of hopelessness
- inappropriate guilt
- feelings of worthlessness
- lack of energy
- poor concentration
- suicidal thoughts
- social withdrawal
- diminished enjoyment of, or interest in, life's normal activities.

When the symptoms of depression are severe, prolonged or impinge on one's quality of life, it is important to seek professional assistance.

The causes of depression are complex and not easy to explain in a few words. However, in very basic terms there are two sources of depression.

First, there is the natural response to events such as retrenchment, significant life changes such as retirement, divorce, or the death of a close friend or relative. This type of depression is sometimes called *reactive depression* because it results from our reaction to an event or an aspect of our lifestyle.

Second, there is depression that comes from the internal chemistry of the brain or from some other organic source. Where such depression has a genetic basis, it is called *endogenous depression.*

Stress/burnout/post-traumatic stress

Stress (psychological)

Psychologically based stress involves feelings of depression and anxiety resulting from one's *perceived inability* to cope with a particular set of circumstances. The words 'perceived inability' are particularly important because what is stressful to one person may not be to another. For example, while some people may find the prospect of running a large multinational organisation stressful, the current Chief Executive Officer may thrive in the role. Similarly, while performing an appendectomy is a routine task for many surgeons, it would be highly stressful for someone without medical training who was forced to operate in an emergency.

'I need to exercise my mind – I think stress is good in my case!'

The person quoted above was actually referring to a phenomenon known as 'facilitating anxiety', that is, the level of pressure we need to motivate ourselves to action. However, the sentiments of what he said are true! Where high-performing individuals are used to working under pressure, they will often report that they find the sudden absence of work pressure to be 'stressful'.

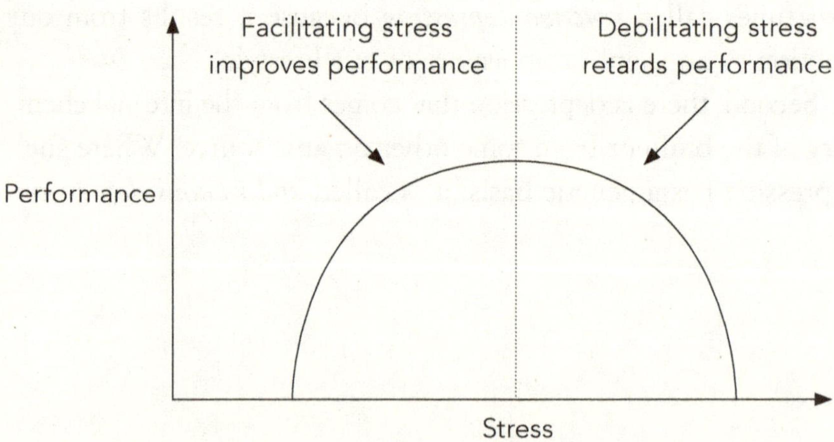

Stress (Physical)

Stress may also be caused by physical conditions such as extreme temperature, high caffeine intake, infection, overexercising, or exposure to some chemicals including alcohol and drugs.

Where both psychological *and* physiological stress are present, the cumulative effects of both can be significant. For example, consider the difference between having to change a tyre on your car when you are running late for an appointment (psychological stress), versus having an entire afternoon to get the job done. If it was also a day when the temperature was over 35 degrees Celsius (physiological stress), you can picture how the two stressors would combine to make the net effect greater than the sum of each stressor.

Burnout

Stress can also occur in the form of burnout, where one becomes overwhelmed from prolonged exposure to a demanding role such as working in a high-pressure job or from caring for a terminally ill loved one.

'I sometimes feel like climbing to the top of a mountain and staying there for about a year. When I eventually came down again, I would start saying "no" to many of those people who keep asking for my services.'

As you can see, this participant on the *Retire 200* project described his reaction to stress in a rather poetic way. His dilemma started when, soon after retirement, he agreed to join the committee of a voluntary organisation. His past business experience, and natural tendency to get things done, resulted in the committee being highly successful and he was soon invited to join other committees. Eventually, he found that he had little time to himself and was actually experiencing a form of work-related stress at a time when he wished to have a more relaxed lifestyle.

Post-traumatic stress

Most people have heard the term 'post-traumatic stress'. This specific type of stress results from exposure to the overwhelming effects of a situation such as arriving home to find your house burned to the ground, or losing all your savings in a recession.

The main factor in common where post-traumatic stress is concerned is that a highly significant or life-threatening event has occurred where the sufferer:

- has little control over the circumstances;
- is not properly trained or prepared to deal with the event;
- is under-resourced with equipment, funds or people.

During the First and Second World Wars, post-traumatic stress was recognised under a number of labels ranging from 'war neurosis' to 'shell shock'. Irrespective of the label, this type of post-traumatic stress was the understandable reaction of *normal* human beings who found themselves immersed in the horror of an *abnormal* situation.

Ways to manage anxiety, depression and stress

Important note: This section of the book is intended to help you develop strategies for managing emotional issues that may be impeding your ability to enjoy life. Consequently, the ideas provided should be seen in the context of 'self-development'.

Where emotional problems such as anxiety or depression are having a serious impact on your lifestyle, or have been present for a long time, or where thoughts of suicide are present, it is important that you seek professional advice from a suitably qualified practitioner.

What steps can I take to feel better right *now*? (Managing the immediate *symptoms* of anxiety, depression and stress)

In this next section we will look at some ideas that have been helpful to others who have experienced anxiety and depression in their lives. Anxiety and depression are two quite different conditions, as we found earlier in this chapter. Because they have different symptoms and triggers, we will treat them separately.

Reducing the symptoms of anxiety

Relaxation, by definition, is the opposite of anxiety. It is, therefore, not surprising that many therapies for reducing anxiety focus on helping people to apply relaxation techniques. If you find that anxiety is affecting your life, taking the time to apply relaxation techniques on a daily basis is highly recommended.

Here are some ideas that you can immediately put into action:

1. BREATHING EXERCISES USING YOUR DIAPHRAGM

The diaphragm is a set of muscles that helps the lungs inflate and deflate. If you look closely at someone who is sleeping, you will see their diaphragm gently rising and falling as they breathe. On the other hand, an anxious person tends to take shallow, rapid breaths. By the conscious use of your diaphragm to breathe deeply and slowly, you will find that your anxiety levels gradually reduce.

To use your diaphragm muscle to breathe deeply:

- Lie down and put your hand on your abdomen (between your navel and your ribcage).

- Breathe in through your nose slowly and deeply. Your hand should rise as you breathe. Send the air far down to the bottom of your lungs. To help do this, try visualising what happens when you fill a bottle with water – the water enters the neck of the bottle and fills from the bottom up. Imagine that your lungs are the bottle and your nose is the opening of the bottle.
- Once you have filled your lungs, wait for a second or two and then breathe out fully through your nose or mouth. As you do this, let the muscles in your arms, legs and face relax so that your entire body is free from tension.
- Complete the above process ten times, remembering to do each round slowly. If you do this for five minutes, you may find that you feel more relaxed.

Note: if you start to feel a little light-headed during the breathing exercises, just stop for a minute or so then recommence.

2. VISUALISATION

When it comes to reducing anxiety, visualisation is a wonderful method of transporting yourself to a peaceful place where you can relax and recharge your batteries. For some, their ideal place may include the sounds of water rushing down a cool stream in the country, or it may be the sounds of the surf crashing onto the sands of a beach. For others, it could be a warm, comfortable room in a luxurious hotel on a snow-covered mountain.

The power of visualisation has long been recognised as a versatile and effective tool by psychologists. For example, athletes having a run of poor performance have been lifted back to their former levels simply by adding visualisation exercises to their training and preparation regimen.

Below is a short example of how I visualise my favourite place in the country where my wife and I go camping by the Acheron River in Buxton, Victoria.

> It is early morning and I am lying under the warm doona in the tent. The cool, fresh air is gently blowing across my face through the tent window. Outside I can hear the sounds of birds marking their territories – the plaintive cry of ravens, the warbling of magpies, and the distant laughter of kookaburras.
>
> Nearby, the water is babbling over the small rocky ledge at the bend in the river as it winds its way down to the sea far away. The gurgling of the water, the gentle breeze rustling the leaves of the gum trees, and the faint smell of the damp charcoal from last night's campfire merge to create the peace and tranquillity I love so much.
>
> While I am immersed in the pleasures of this wonderful place I am breathing slowly and deeply – I feel relaxed, happy and peaceful.

Have a think about *your* ideal place, and then imagine yourself there taking it all in. If there is no actual place that you know of, invent one – it really does not matter. Write a description of what it is like and include not just the physical setting but the sounds you hear, the smells, what you are touching, how warm it is. Use as many of the five senses as possible when writing your description.

If you like, you can record yourself describing the scene so that you can lie back and play it when you are relaxing. You could also record the instructions for diaphragmatic breathing first so that your recording takes you on a relaxing journey starting with the breathing exercises and ending at your favourite peaceful scene. There are many meditation apps available for smartphone users that can assist with visualisation and breathing.

Reducing the symptoms of depression

'Life is boring – when I was alive I did things – now life is a living death with nothing to look forward to.'

When people are depressed they often experience what is known as the 'cognitive triad', that is, they have an unrealistically negative view of:

1. themselves
2. their environment
3. their future.

The person quoted above was clearly very depressed when we spoke. If you look at what they said, you see the clear signs of the cognitive triad. If you are depressed and have been for a long time, it is wise to seek professional help. Depending on the type of depression you are experiencing, different types of therapy, including medication, may be required.

If you are presently suffering from depression and it is:

- relatively short lived,
- not causing you major problems such as suicidal thoughts,
- related to a specific event such as adjusting to your lifestyle in retirement,

the following suggestions may be helpful.

1. ACTION: DOING SOMETHING IS BETTER THAN DOING NOTHING

When someone is depressed, the prospect of performing simple actions, such as telephoning a friend, may be more then they can bear contemplating. It can be at times such as this that well-meaning friends or relatives may advise them to 'get out and do something' or to join a club and meet people. If you are presently depressed, you will know just how annoying and deflating such well-meaning advice can be.

On the other hand, evidence from clinical studies demonstrates that taking small steps, such as getting out of the house and going up the street, or walking through the park, can help to relieve the symptoms of depression. It is certainly more uplifting than deciding to sit around and do nothing, even though this may seem preferable at the time.

2. FOCUS ON WHAT YOU ARE DOING RATHER THAN ON YOUR DEPRESSION

One of the reasons that action is more beneficial than inaction is that it provides you with the opportunity to take your mind off your depression, even if this is only for a short time. To maximise the benefit of any actions you take, try to focus your attention on the details of what you are doing, rather than on your depression. For example, if you are window shopping, focus on aspects of the products such as their colour, design . . . and begin to push your feelings of depression into the background.

3. LOOK AT WHAT HAS WORKED IN THE PAST

If your depression is relatively recent, you will be able to recall times when you took part in activities that you found interesting and enjoyable. Look back to these times when you were not depressed and make a list of the actions that you once found fun. You may find that as you develop your list, the activities do not seem to sound as enjoyable to you now as they once did. This is all part of the cognitive triad mentioned earlier. Notwithstanding this, set yourself the goal of undertaking one of these activities within a defined time frame, for example, within one week. Take small steps at first and then, as you gain confidence, gradually increase your activities.

If your depression is due to the death of someone close, and you find that your list of activities includes things you used to do with your deceased friend or partner, you may be saying, 'But it won't be as much fun now without them'. While this is probably true, it is still likely that involvement in the activity will be more beneficial than just staying home and doing nothing.

Reducing the symptoms of stress

The symptoms of stress are often close to those of anxiety. Consequently, many of the techniques that are used to successfully reduce anxiety can also help you to reduce your levels of stress.

If your stress results from a physical stressor such as substance abuse, you should seek professional advice regarding how to manage the problem. It is important to remember that, in certain cases, it is dangerous to simply 'go cold turkey' by just ceasing to take a drug. The group of drugs known as benzodiazepines, which includes brand names such as Valium and Serapax, are examples of drugs that should only be withdrawn under medical supervision.

In cases where stress is caused by exposure to a particular environment or lifestyle, withdrawal from the situation is one solution. If this is not a practical option then relaxation exercises can help you through your stressful time.

What steps can I take to manage the *causes* of anxiety, depression and stress?

In this next section we are going to look at a model used by psychologists when helping people deal with issues that impact on their wellbeing. The model is called Rational-Emotive Therapy (RET) and is well established as a successful therapeutic process. RET is used successfully for treating problems ranging from simple phobias to serious cases of depression and anxiety.

Note: As in the majority of psychotherapies, Rational Emotive Therapy is not necessarily a 'one-stop-shop' for all problems. In any case, it is best applied in conjunction with a relevant professional who will guide you through the process.

Rational Emotive Therapy (RET)

Put simply, RET works on the basis that emotional problems such as anxiety and depression are often the by-product of the irrational or illogical beliefs that we have about ourselves and the world around us. In other words, it is not *what* happens to us (for example, 'My car was stolen') that makes us angry, sad or depressed, but rather what we *say to ourselves* about what has happened ('This is terrible – I cannot stand it'). Where our belief system and self-talk are irrational or illogical, our emotional reactions to events will also be dysfunctional ('Because I cannot stand it, I am *depressed*').

When people are being introduced to RET for the first time, they sometimes find the term 'irrational' offensive. However, it is important to remember that in the context of RET, 'irrational' does not imply mental illness. Rather, it describes our tendency to let our feelings and behaviours be ruled by the untested, unproven beliefs that we all have, and which can cause us unnecessary anxiety or depression.

The goal of RET is to therefore show people how to re-examine their thoughts, belief systems and self-talk so that they can then challenge and dispute the validity of any irrational or illogical beliefs they discover. The next step is to replace these irrational beliefs with rational alternatives.

RET practitioners refer to the 'ABCs' of RET. These are described on the following page:

[A] First, there is an '**<u>A</u>**ctivating' event, that is, the thing that happens to us, for example, 'I lost the part-time job I found soon after I retired.'

[B] Second, our '**<u>B</u>**elief system' interprets the event, for example, 'This is terrible, without this job I am a worthless person.'

[C] Third, we experience the emotional '**<u>C</u>**onsequences' of our interpretation, for example, 'Because I believe this is "terrible" and because I believe that I am a "worthless" person I now become depressed, anxious and sad.'

Here is an example of how untested irrational beliefs can have an impact on our wellbeing. Let us imagine that John has just come home from his PROBUS club and is reflecting on an experience he had there today.

A = **Activating event**		**B =** **Belief system**		**C =** **Consequences**
'Today I was snubbed by Colin, the club president and the most popular member of the club.'	+	'Because Colin likes most members of the club, I am obviously *terribly boring*. This situation is *awful* and *I can't stand it*. Clearly, I am a *worthless* person and *must* resign from the club.'	=	'I feel *bitter, angry, rejected* and *depressed*.'

You can probably already see the irrational beliefs that are causing John's distress. Apart from the fact that Colin's 'snub' might have been unintentional, there are real flaws in the logic of John's belief system.

Let us try it again after John has challenged the validity of his irrational beliefs and replaced them with rational alternatives.

A = **Activating event**		B = **Belief system**		C = **Consequences**
'Today Colin, the most popular member of the club, failed to acknowledge me when I greeted him.'	+	'Either Colin did not hear me, or is in a bad mood, or simply does not like me. If Colin does not like me this is *unfortunate*, because I like him. However, the fact that he may not like me does not mean that I am worthless, unlikeable or a failure.'	=	'I feel *disappointed* and would *prefer* that Colin liked me. I am *saddened* and *a little annoyed* by this possibility, but not depressed.'

You can see from the above example that John's response is more logical and stands up to scrutiny. Instead of a terrible situation that he can't stand and which renders him a worthless person, the more rational John regards the situation realistically as unfortunate. Instead of feeling bitter, angry, rejected and depressed, John is disappointed and would prefer that he was accepted. Consequently he is now saddened and annoyed rather than depressed.

The ten most common irrational beliefs

Most cognitive psychologists agree that we *all* have a number of irrational beliefs that we need to regularly challenge and modify if we are to lead happy, fulfilling lives. Albert Ellis, the founder of Rational Emotive Therapy, argued that there are ten commonly recurring irrational beliefs that he encountered among his clients during his many years of psychological practice.

Irrational Belief Number One: 'I must have the love and approval of all the people I find significant.'
Rational Alternative: We all *desire* and *want* the approval of others and would be *less happy* without it. However, we do not *need* the approval of others. Saying that we *need* it implies that we would shrivel up and die without it.

Irrational Belief Number Two: 'I must be competent or talented in some significant area of life.'
Rational Alternative: While it would be *pleasant* to be talented and competent at something, it is not critically important. The problem with Irrational Belief Number Two is that it is often associated with the belief that you are what you do – for example, I *am* a doctor. In fact, nobody *is* a doctor. Some people work *as* a doctor – but they may also work *as* a parent and *as* a grower of prize roses.

Irrational Belief Number Three: 'When people act unfairly or nastily, they are bad people who should be punished.'
Rational Alternative: Ask yourself, 'Where is it written that so-and-so *shouldn't* behave in this manner to you? Where is the proof that they *mustn't* act this way?' It would be *preferable* that they didn't act as they do, but hardly *essential*.

Irrational Belief Number Four: 'When things do not go the way I would like them to, it is awful, horrible and terrible, and I can't stand it.'
Rational Alternative: Although it may be *unfortunate* or *unpleasant* when things do not work out the way you would like them to, you *can* stand it. It may be less than what you want, and consequently regretful, but you *can* stand it.

Irrational Belief Number Five: 'Emotional misery and distress come from external sources and I have no ability to control or change my feelings.'
Rational Alternative: Much of the pain other people or events allegedly 'cause' us results from us taking rejection or criticism too seriously. We tell ourselves that we *cannot stand it* when some people do not approve of us, and that life is *totally worthless* without their approval. However, if you examine this thinking further it is clear you will not cease to exist if your next-door neighbours suddenly indicate that they prefer the company of others.

You can, therefore, modify your thinking to something like: 'I would *greatly prefer* that my neighbours like me and would feel *much more comfortable* with this situation. However, if they are determined to dislike me, *I can stand it* even though *I don't like it*.'

Irrational Belief Number Six: 'If something seems dangerous or to be feared I must be preoccupied with it, dwell on it possibly occurring, and become anxious about it.'
Rational Alternative: If something is dangerous then we can take action to avoid it where possible. If there is nothing we can do about it, we can stop ourselves from the self-defeating practice of exaggerating its effects and making ourselves miserable. For example, if you live near the rainforests of Queensland, there will be deadly taipan snakes in the area. However, constantly dwelling on the possibility of being bitten by one of them would be unhelpful.

Irrational Belief Number Seven: 'It is easier to avoid many of life's difficulties and responsibilities than to apply self-discipline.'
Rational Alternative: When we avoid our responsibilities, we are usually exaggerating the level of difficulty and discomfort they involve. We may also be afraid of trying in case we fail. However, failing is a natural part of the continual learning process we all experience. It can be helpful to remember that most experts in a

particular skill have only become proficient by repeatedly doing it poorly and failing many times.

Irrational Belief Number Eight: 'My past is all-important – because something once strongly influenced my life, it will go on determining my feelings and behaviour now.'
Rational Alternative: By allowing yourself to blame past experiences for today's feelings and behaviours, you are actually taking the easy way out by not seeking new solutions to your problems. If you continue to act in a certain way just because you have done so in the past, you deny yourself new experiences that may bring new rewards and solutions.

Irrational Belief Number Nine: 'People and things should turn out better than they are – it is awful and horrible when you do not find solutions to life's hard realities.'
Rational Alternative: There is no compelling reason why anyone or anything *should* be better just because you want this to be the case. While it would be *preferable* if things were better, we are just displaying a childishly low tolerance for frustration when we say, 'Things *should* be better and *I can't stand it* when they are not!'

Irrational Belief Number Ten: 'I can obtain maximum happiness in life by doing as little as possible and by concentrating on enjoying myself to the full.'
Rational Alternative: Most people find that they need to be doing something active and to be goal oriented. Sitting around doing nothing may be fine when you are on a holiday – however, doing nothing all the time rarely suits intelligent people.

How many of the top ten irrational beliefs were among yours?

How do I apply RET to my life?

First, identify the situations that cause you to feel anxious or upset. Make a list of them on the left-hand side of a sheet of paper. Such events may include those of the type described in the 'top ten' above, or may relate to your own specific issues.

Second, try to identify what upsets you about the event. What are you saying to yourself about the event? Do you hear extreme terms like 'must never', or 'I can't stand it', or 'they should always . . .'? Write your self-talk down on the right-hand side of the paper next to the situations that cause you anxiety or depression. Where you detect unprovable, illogical self-talk, you will need to modify it to a more logical alternative.

Finally, once you believe you have modified your irrational beliefs and self-talk to more rational alternatives, try imagining the event that was causing you distress. Listen to your new, modified self-talk, and estimate the effect the event now has on you. Do you feel better about the event? If not, you may need to revisit your beliefs and self-talk again.

Some readers may be asking themselves right now, 'But if my self-talk is so faulty or illogical, how will I know?' It's a good question! For RET, and indeed most psychotherapies, to work effectively it is advisable to use a professional counsellor such as a psychologist to help us challenge our irrational self-talk. Just leaving this task to ourselves encourages our natural tendency to deny the existence or magnitude of personal problems.

I can't afford a psychologist – how can I maximise the effectiveness of RET on my own?

The imaginary panel

One idea that can help increase the likely effectiveness of RET, without the presence of a psychologist, is to first think of three compassionate, intelligent people whom you greatly respect. They may still be living, or may be people from the past such as a teacher or relative. Work through the three steps for applying RET (above), but use your imaginary 'panel' of wise and caring people to assess your self-talk. What do you think their reactions would be to your self-talk?

Say it aloud

Another way to test the logic of your self-talk is to say it aloud to yourself. Does your self-talk sound as logical when spoken aloud as it did when you were just thinking it?

Write down your self-talk and contrast it with rational alternatives

Here is an example:

Irrational (what you are saying to yourself now)	Rational (your written rational alternative)
'I *always* get nervous when asked to speak at my PROBUS club. I *can't stand it* and I know I will *never* be any good at it.'	'*So far*, I have found that public speaking makes me *very nervous*. However, there is no reason why this should continue if I seek help, for example, by joining a public speaking group such as Rostrum.'

When you find that certain events or situations upset you, draw a table like the one above and write down your present self-talk with a rational alternative. This process will help you modify your irrational self-talk.

Some examples of using RET to change irrational beliefs or self-talk

Irrational	Rational
'It would be awful/terrible if I did not get elected president of the club.'	'It would be very disappointing if I did not get the presidency but it would hardly be the end of the world.'
'I am no good at arithmetic and I'll never be able to work out my tax return.'	'So far, I have not performed well at arithmetic, but that does not mean that with some help I cannot improve in the future.'
'I am a hopeless failure at social functions.'	'I have sometimes performed poorly at social functions, but with some work and advice I will be able to improve.'
'Living on the pension is killing me – I must have a high standard of living because when I don't, I can't bear it.'	'I would very much like to have a higher standard of living and I get annoyed that I don't. However, I can bear it and can adjust to it.'

You can see from these examples that much of our faulty thinking and belief system results from our tendency:

1. TO CATASTROPHISE SITUATIONS – FOR EXAMPLE:

   'I was twenty minutes late for my luncheon appointment with Sue today and she was clearly very annoyed. I will probably lose her friendship now and eventually will have no friends left at all.'

2. TO FALL VICTIM TO *I-CAN'T-STAND-IT-ITIS* – FOR EXAMPLE:

   'When people are rude to me I can't stand it and believe that they should be punished.'

3. TO ALLOW EXTREME WORDS SUCH AS *NEVER* AND *CAN'T*, AS WELL AS DIRECTIVES SUCH AS *SHOULDN'T*, *COULDN'T* AND *MUSTN'T* BECOME PART OF OUR THINKING AND SELF-TALK – FOR EXAMPLE:

> *'I'll never be able to get up and address the members of the club – I always get nervous and I can't stand it when people see me like that!'*

SUMMARY:

In this chapter we . . .

- Discovered why some people suffer from emotional problems in retirement.
- Examined the differences between anxiety, depression and stress.
- Discovered ways to relieve the symptoms of a range of emotional problems.
- Examined ways in which we can apply the principles of Rational Emotive Therapy to modify the faulty self-talk that can cause us to be anxious, stressed or depressed.

CHECKLIST

- ☐ I now understand the differences between anxiety, depression and stress.
- ☐ I know how to apply diaphragmatic breathing to reduce anxiety and stress.
- ☐ I know how to use visualisation to reduce anxiety and stress.
- ☐ I understand the importance of taking small active steps to reduce depression.
- ☐ I understand how Rational Emotive Therapy can help reduce feelings of depression, anxiety and stress.
- ☐ I have used Rational Emotive Therapy to work on one area of my life that causes me to become anxious, stressed or depressed.

CHAPTER EIGHT

Building and maintaining your self-esteem

AIMS OF THIS CHAPTER

- To examine the relationship between how we view ourselves (our self-concept) and our attitude towards ourselves (self-esteem).
- To identify the causes and effects of low self-esteem.
- To examine ways of building self-esteem to increase our enjoyment of life.

What is self-esteem?

Self-esteem can be described as the sum of our levels of self-respect and self-acceptance. Self-esteem affects the way we behave, think and feel.

- When we are suffering from low self-esteem we find that we are depressed, anxious and lack self-confidence. Consequently, we may go through life short-changing ourselves by denying our natural abilities and our right to realise our full potential.
- Conversely, when we have healthy levels of self-esteem, we also have healthy levels of self-respect. We open ourselves to more of life's options because we correctly believe that we deserve them.

Behaviours of people with low self-esteem

Here are some of the behaviours that may be found in people who have low levels of self-esteem.

- *They may have trouble saying no*: Lack of belief in themselves leads people with low self-esteem to want to please others as a way of gaining acceptance.
- *They may find it difficult to accept a compliment graciously*: Because their self-esteem is low, they do not believe they are worthy of the compliments they may receive.
- *They may take little care with their appearance and grooming*: They may believe that attending to grooming will make little difference because they 'know' they are unlikeable or unattractive anyway. Lack of care with grooming may also be a by-product of the depression that can accompany low self-esteem.
- *They fear rejection from their peers and others*: Because their belief in themselves is already fragile, they believe that others

will reject them and, therefore, they withdraw from social interaction before this can occur.

- *They find it difficult to list their positive points*: Because their self-concept is low, they may not believe that they have positive aspects to their personality or appearance.
- *They may make regular self-disparaging comments about themselves, their abilities, their appearance*: In some cases this is a strategy to stop others from 'getting in first' with hurtful criticisms. In other cases, it is done in the hope that others will disagree with their criticism and bolster their self-esteem by saying something like, 'No! You're not really overweight!'

Self-esteem – feelings and behaviours based on our self-concept

Our level of self-esteem is dependent on our self-concept, that is, the way in which we perceive ourselves. Self-concept may be broken down into seven subsets:

1. *Intellectual self-concept*: The way we rate ourselves as we compare our thinking ability, or our intelligence, to that of our peers and others around us.
2. *Personal self-concept*: How we evaluate our personality and our sense of adequacy when we compare ourselves to others around us.
3. *Social self-concept*: How we perceive our skills at social interaction compared to those of other people with whom we socialise.
4. *Family self-concept*: Our perception of ourselves when we examine our worth or contribution as a family member.
5. *Physical self-concept*: How we perceive our physical condition compared to others – the way we look, our state of health and our sexuality.

6. *Moral self-concept*: How we rate ourselves based on our personal ethics or moral code. For some people this also includes their relationship with their religion and their consequent self-rating as a 'good' or 'bad' individual.
7. *Behavioural-action self-concept*: How we rate ourselves based on our behaviours and activities, for example, our perceptions of ourselves as lazy versus diligent, constructive versus destructive . . .

Interestingly, aspects of self-concept adversely affecting one person can impact quite differently on the self-esteem of another person. For example, an obese teenage girl may be distressed about her body shape because the messages she receives daily from the media, her peers and members of her family continually reinforce the idea that being fat is not 'cool'. On the other hand, an overweight opera singer may not care about his obesity. His high levels of self-esteem may be dependent on his ability to use his talent, and on the adulation he receives from his audience. Similarly, a sumo wrestler may actually regard his obesity positively due to its high levels of acceptance among his peers and fans.

The good news for us all is that self-esteem influenced by aspects of our negative self-concept can be counterbalanced by self-esteem based on positive aspects of our self-concept. Consequently, if someone is embarrassed by being overweight they can still enjoy a high level of self-esteem by focusing on their intellectual or artistic abilities.

How our self-concept is formed

Much of our self-concept is shaped by the influences of the adults in our lives when our personalities were developing. At this time, when we were dependent on our parents, grandparents, and teachers, our self-worth or self-concept was influenced by the quality and consistency of the positive feedback they provided us. If we were lucky and were surrounded by nurturing adults, we had a good chance of emerging from childhood with a well-rounded, healthy self-concept.

Below are seven broad areas where childhood exposure to adults has an impact on the formation of self-concept. Once we have looked at these influences we will look at ways of rebuilding or repairing our self-esteem as adults.

1. Highly critical or demanding parents/teachers

Naturally, parents should encourage their children to perform at their best and to take pride in their achievements. However, if parents set standards for their children that are too high, their children are destined to fail repeatedly. For example, some parents put undue pressure on their child to come first in the class or to excel at sport. In many instances, these parents are attempting to relive their own lives through their children and in doing so unwittingly impose immense psychological pressure on them. Such experiences can leave children feeling defeated and guilty as they struggle to succeed when the odds are stacked against them. Moreover, because children usually have no way of knowing that the demands being placed on them are unreasonable, they naturally assume that *they* are at fault when they do not live up to their parents' expectations.

2. Children of famous or very successful parents

Children of highly successful parents can also fall victim to low self-concept. Where a parent is an outstanding success, particularly in a highly visible setting such as business, sport or the arts, it is very difficult for the child to compare their own endeavours favourably. The problem can be compounded if the parent is frequently absent due to the demands their success makes on them. This further deprives the child of the consistent positive reinforcement and nurturing they require.

3. Exposure to strict codes of behaviour

Negative influences on a child's self-concept can occur in an environment that prescribes certain behaviours as good, and proscribes others as bad or 'sinful'. A common feature of these settings occurs when the child's successes are regarded as a 'gift from God' for which the child should be 'thankful'. However, when the child fails it is attributed to their laziness or to some other personal deficit. In such an environment the child is in a no-win situation, denied positive self-esteem for their successes but blamed for their failures.

4. Abusive parents/teachers

Children who have been physically or sexually abused by adults often find that they have an array of confused feelings including guilt, personal inadequacy, rage, insecurity and the inability to trust others. Where trust is diminished, people risk becoming emotionally isolated, which leads to poor self-concept and attendant low self-esteem.

At the heart of child abuse is the shattering of children's natural preparedness to trust that adults are safe. Tragically, those who prey on children often manoeuvre themselves into positions of trust or authority where the child may actually be encouraged by their parents to place their trust in the very person abusing them.

5. Abandonment

A healthy self-concept is established within an environment of care and positive reinforcement. However, if children feel abandoned by their parents they may regard themselves as not important enough to be loved. Abandonment can take a number of forms. Sometimes it involves literal separation – on other occasions, it is a case of psychological abandonment. Some examples follow:

- The parent rejects the child. Rejection may take the form of being fostered or adopted out of the family, or it may be rejection in the form of coldness or indifference on the part of one or both of the parents. In some cases, the parent may be attempting to manage personal problems such as depression or physical illness. In these cases, it may simply be beyond their emotional resources to attend to their child while dealing with their own illness and the concurrent financial problems that are often a by-product of such situations.
- There can also be cases of 'psychological' abandonment, for example, where the mother and father are very young themselves they may find the unrelenting demands of child rearing too much to handle. This problem is compounded when a single parent is raising the child alone or is required to subsist on a single parent's government welfare.
- The effect of divorce on children has been the subject of numerous studies on the comparative benefits to the child of staying in a disruptive, unhappy home compared with living with one parent and seeing the other periodically. In either case the child is often on the perimeter of their parents' disputes and acrimony, and may form the opinion that *they* are in some way to blame for their parents' distress.
- Finally, there is the sense of abandonment in childhood that accompanies the death of a parent. Where the child is very young they may have difficulty understanding why a parent has left them to 'go to Heaven' and may feel that they have been abandoned. The sense of abandonment can then be compounded by the changes in the household environment as the surviving parent attempts to raise the child while managing their own grief under difficult circumstances.

6. Parents with addictions

Without a reliable and consistent environment children become confused and insecure. Where parents are addicted to alcohol or drugs they are rarely able to provide a stable environment. Consequently, behaviour of the child's that is applauded and encouraged one day when everyone is drunk or high may be condemned and result in corporal punishment the next time the parents are hungover or withdrawing from a substance. Naturally, this unpredictable environment causes children to lose confidence in their own judgement.

Where hard drugs are involved, the parents invariably associate with other addicts who may be the only other people who understand and tolerate their behaviour. Consequently, the child receives mixed messages as they grapple to manage the chaos and instability at home on one hand, and the structured, predictable life they experience at school.

At a psychological level the child sees their addicted parent(s) denying the problem of their addiction and may also learn that denying their own feelings is the best strategy to use to deal with their own pain and confusion.

7. Overindulgent parents

Most of us can remember childhood peers who were 'spoiled rotten'. It seemed that they were the luckiest kids we knew. They always got what they wanted for birthdays and Christmas and always seemed to have the latest toys or clothes. The problem for such children, however, is that they may never learn to postpone pleasant events. As a result, in adulthood they can find life immensely frustrating if they cannot get what they want NOW! The major risks associated with such conditioning are boredom with the drabness of life, or financial disasters caused by the inability to defer purchasing desired goods on credit or to manage money appropriately.

Retirement and self-esteem

The changes to our lifestyle that follow retirement can impact both positively and negatively on our self-esteem. Many of the participants on the *Retire 200* program were relieved to hear that that they were not alone when it came to being negatively affected by retirement. In particular, some people felt embarrassed about admitting that they missed the status of their job. One participant described his dilemma in this way:

'Over the years I have got into the habit of asking people that I am being introduced to about what line of work they are in. It has always been a good ice-breaker for me, especially since I was proud of my own occupation as manager of an engineering section of BHP. Soon after retirement, I found that I felt awkward when meeting people because I had lost my old patter. It really knocked my self-confidence around for a while.'

The *Retire 200* raised eleven aspects of retirement that impacted on self-esteem. We will look briefly at these now, and then examine ways to boost self-esteem should this be an issue for you.

1. Loss of identity

'It is so easy to describe yourself as "unimportant" because you are not working or earning money.'

'You must view yourself as "'somebody".'

Some people describe themselves as being devalued by not having a role to play in the workforce. Psychologists frequently encounter this problem, not just with those in retirement, but with those who have lost their jobs due to organisational closure, retrenchment or ill health. From a psychological point of view, the person may be identifying with the job. For example, instead of saying, 'I work *as* an engineer', a person may say, 'I *am* an engineer'. Where such faulty logic is used, the corollary is that in retirement, 'I am a nothing'!

2. Loss of status

Where a retired person's former role comprised a high-status occupation such as the Chief Executive Officer or the National Sales Manager, they not only lose their career but also the status provided by their organisational title and its benefits.

3. Loss of purpose

For many people, going to work each day provides them with a purpose in life, such as:

- Making a worthwhile contribution at work.
- Interacting with colleagues.
- Contributing to the financial welfare of their family.

4. Loss of structure

People who have found security from working in highly structured environments may suffer a loss of self-esteem if they find themselves locked into a comparatively aimless lifestyle soon after retiring.

There are a number of ways of establishing structure in retirement. Probably the simplest and most widely used is maintaining a diary or wall planner that you fill with events and appointments. These events can range from having lunch with a friend to attending meetings or the annual general meetings of organisations in which you have shares.

5. Social stereotypes

The impact of social stereotypes can impinge on the self-esteem of those who have retired, especially those who do so at a comparatively young age. The work ethic in Australia and New Zealand is such that society often questions the moral strength of those who are not gainfully employed. In many cases, such judgemental attitudes are inappropriate yet still affect people who may have no logical reason to feel guilty. The work ethic is so entrenched in some people that even when they are retired they still feel guilty if they are not doing something constructive. One participant on the *Retire 200* program could not bring himself to turn on the television set during the day because this represented idleness to him. Others felt inappropriately guilty accepting the age pension because they viewed it as a handout rather than the benefit that was being funded by their years of paying income tax.

6. Reduction in income

Very few people are able to generate the same levels of income that they enjoyed during their working life. Consequently, lifestyle adjustments usually need to be made if financial resources are to last. People who had planned for their retirement, and who had agreed together how to adjust their spending patterns before retirement, were usually much better off emotionally than those who had not planned. The latter tended to wake up to the realisation that they were going to need to reduce spending far more than they had anticipated. For example, the former practice of going to a restaurant once a week may now not be possible. Self-esteem can take a battering under these circumstances, particularly if dining out has been with a group of friends who can continue to afford it.

7. Loss of important social networks

In every organisation, there are people who are prepared to dedicate much of their spare time to organising social events for staff. These events may range from raffles and other fundraising ideas for charities, to playing the role of Father Christmas at the office party. Notwithstanding the payoff to the organisation from increased morale and team building, these natural organisers thoroughly enjoy their roles. On retiring, it is important that such people quickly capitalise on their skills as organisers by establishing themselves as active members of clubs or voluntary organisations.

8. Changed relationships

The relationship between partners is usually affected when one or both retire. Roles such as doing the shopping or mowing the lawn might have been designated on the basis that the balance between the rigours of a career and home maintenance needed to be fairly distributed. (The arguments reported by *Retire 200* participants over what constituted 'fair' distribution of duties would fill a book on its own!) However, when both partners are retired and at home all day, the lines between who should do what can blur.

9. Lack of activity

The need for Purposeful Activities is addressed in detail in Chapter One. However, it is clear that when retired people are not involved in sufficient hours of Purposeful Activity each week, they are at risk from anxiety, depression and stress, any one of which can have an impact on their levels of self-esteem.

10. Substance abuse

In many cases, substance abuse is simply the by-product of boredom or loneliness. Seeking refuge in alcohol or drugs can be a significant risk factor when people are living alone. Former drinking habits may gradually change from enjoying one or two glasses of wine with dinner to commencing drinking earlier in the day. As alcohol is a depressant, such drinkers may find that lethargy and alcohol-related illnesses can lead to the abuse of painkillers. One of the first casualties of such addiction is self-esteem.

11. Destructive pastimes (for example, gambling)

Several people on the *Retire 200* research raised the issue of problem gambling. Like substance abuse, gambling problems often start because of boredom or loneliness.

Gambling includes the following activities:

- **Betting:** Where bets are placed on a race.
- **Gaming:** Where money is wagered on the result of a game such as cards or roulette.
- **Lotteries:** Where money purchases numbers to be drawn from a pool.

The proliferation of gambling outlets has made those with a gambling problem, or suffering from boredom, a likely target. In recent times the gaming industry has identified women as a growth market and now strategically designs their venues to provide a safe and entertaining environment.

Self-esteem is affected by gambling in a number of ways. However, two significant areas that were raised by those on the *Retire 200* program were:

(a) The impacts on financial health when the main earning years are over. Guilt and despair follow as losses are chased and more money is diverted from retirement savings.
(b) The compulsive nature of gambling causes reductions in self-esteem where gamblers view themselves as being locked into a habit that is beyond their control.

Ways to improve your self-esteem

Challenge the voices from the past

If you think back to your childhood, you may be able to recall the types of criticisms that you received from teachers, parents, and your peers. Make a list of the negative or hurtful comments that you recall people saying and which still bother you. Take a piece of paper and write the comments on one side of the paper. Then counter them with your own comments on the other side.

Some examples of how to reject the voices from the past are shown below. Develop your own list and read it when you are feeling down.

'You are lazy . . .'	*'I am not lazy. I work long and hard in certain areas of my life. However, I do have quite different priorities in life to [Mary, John . . .], which may be giving them the impression that I am lazy.'*
'You are dumb . . .'	*'I may not live up to [Sue, Peter . . .]'s expectations in some ways. However, intelligence and common sense take a number of forms. I believe I have made many intelligent decisions in my life.'*

'You are vain . . .'	*'I take pride in my appearance because I enjoy looking good and feeling good about myself. I also believe that grooming is important [in business, to set an example for my children . . .]. If some people interpret the way I attend to my grooming as vanity, I cannot be concerned about their views.'*
'You are a failure . . .'	*'It is true that a number of aspects of my life have not turned out as well as I would have liked. However, there is a big difference between failing and being a "failure". Furthermore, part of the reason I sometimes fail is my preparedness to try new ideas. If people don't try anything new they can't fail at it! However, I would rather keep on trying even if it means I continue to fail from time to time.'*

Building self-esteem through group membership

'You need emotional support if you are unmarried and do not have close family – for me it is belonging to my church.'

Some people gain comfort and social support from belonging to a religious group and described a deep sense of spiritual belonging and comfort from their religious beliefs. Others were less religious but valued membership of a church because of the social life, and the network of caring people who were there for each other in times of need.

The shoebox method of building self-esteem

Some years ago, a convention relating to self-esteem and motivation was held in Melbourne. One of the platform speakers was an insurance salesman who, after many years in the industry, had risen to the top of the sales ladder. It had been no easy feat. As we listened, he described the rejection he experienced ten to twenty times a day as he approached prospective clients hoping to discuss their insurance needs. Can you imagine what it would be like to be rejected, often rudely, day in and day out, year after year?

During the speech, this hardened sales veteran held up a battered shoebox and described to the audience the role it played in his ability to remain motivated in such a harsh psychological environment. In the shoebox were scraps of paper on which were written the details of achievements and events of which he was proud. Included in the box was a letter of thanks from the widow of a former client whose insurance policy had paid out a mortgage. There were also notes of thanks for the talks he had given to clubs and schools, and a birthday card made for him by his five-year-old granddaughter.

Every time this salesman felt demotivated, he would sit down with the shoebox and read the contents to energise himself. As new positive experiences occurred in his life he would write them down on scraps of paper and add them to the box. He claimed that the process of reading the contents of his shoebox never failed to rejuvenate him. Many of my clients now successfully use the shoebox technique during times when they are feeling down.

Generating a list of your good points

In the shoebox method we saw how you can keep a record of communications from others who have recognised your achievements. For some of us, however, this may be a difficult task. We may not move in circles where we are likely to attract the sort of public attention that results in testimonials. We may also be quiet achievers who simply do not draw attention to ourselves, or we may possess the types of qualities that do not attract letters, cards, and acclaim. If this is true in your case, there is still much you can do without the input of others. Try asking yourself questions such as the ones that follow – then supply your own responses:

Some questions you can use	Your answers
'Am I a good friend to anyone?'	
'Am I loyal?'	
'Who are the people who like me?' (If some of these people are now deceased, still include them.)	
'Am I punctual?'	
'Am I well organised?'	
'What do I do well at home?'	

Some questions you can use	Your answers
'What do I do well when I am with my friends?'	
'What was something my best friend at school liked about me?'	
'What do my children, grandchildren and friends like about me?'	
'What do I like about my looks?'	
'How have I ever managed my way through a difficult time in the past?'	
'Do I have a good sense of humour?'	
'Do I try new things from time to time?'	
'Do I have a nice laugh?'	

Try adding your own questions (especially if you think you may have a good answer).

When you have generated your list and can think of no more questions, turn the ones with positive answers around and make them statements. For example, if the answer to 'Am I loyal?' is 'Yes', then write down 'I am loyal because I . . .' Continue to write down statements for all the questions with positive answers and make up your own 'shoebox' to put them in. As you think of other good aspects of your personality, appearance or behaviours, add them to the shoebox. Make sure you keep them handy to read when you are feeling down.

Twelve ideas for building your self-esteem

Here are some ideas that you can apply to build your levels of self-esteem.

1. Accept yourself for who you are

We all have strengths and weaknesses. Before we can improve our areas of weakness we need to accept ourselves as fallible human beings. Then, once we start to feel okay about ourselves we will find that we are more likely to take risks and to 'have a go' at change.

2. Forgive yourself

We have all said and done things in the past that we regret. However, the 'past has passed'. Instead of dwelling on how it could have been, regard your mistakes as opportunities to learn and grow. If there are areas of your past life that continue to cause you regret or distress, do something positive or helpful for someone *now* to balance the wrong you believe you are responsible for in the past.

3. Understand and forgive the imperfections of others

When we discussed the origins of self-concept earlier in this chapter, you may have found yourself getting angry as you recalled aspects of your own childhood. Go back and think about the influences that may have caused those around you to be less than perfect. Think about the resources and help *they* may have lacked in their own lives and try to empathise with their situation. If you can't forgive them, at least try to understand that their actions were based on their own ignorance, lack of skill or personal deficits.

4. Don't just rely on external influences to feel good

If someone rejects you, or behaves in a way that upsets you, focus your attention back on who you are. Remember your own good points and the positive things that you have achieved in your life such as making someone happy, listening to a friend who needed to talk, or helping someone in distress.

5. Do something to be proud of

Add up your achievements like the salesman with the shoebox. Everyone has achieved something positive during their life. For example, once when I was volunteering as a Lifeline telephone counsellor, a young woman told me how she had walked to the local railway line with the intention of throwing herself under a train. She was suffering from severe depression associated with a psychiatric disorder, had no job, no friends, and had been rejected by her family. On the way to the railway line she happened to pass a woman who smiled at her as their paths crossed. That simple act of pleasantness gave the young woman the strength to go on living for another day. So it is possible that we have all had a positive effect on others without even being aware of it.

6. Look after yourself

If you are overtired or out of condition, you are more likely to become anxious and insecure, which in turn will impact negatively on your self-esteem. Try to get enough sleep, balance your diet and exercise regularly.

7. Accept your mistakes

Regard your mistakes as opportunities for growth. If you make a mistake do not try to pretend it has not happened or attempt to pass the blame on to others. Accept your mistakes and learn from them. Try to find ways to avoid similar mistakes in the future. Be prepared to say 'I don't know', rather than bluffing your way through situations.

8. Set and attain some realistic goals

Achieving goals is one of the most satisfying accomplishments that we can experience. In the chapter on personality we examine why some people are more naturally inclined to set goals than others. However, regardless of your natural tendency, you will find that setting goals, and then achieving them, does wonders for your self-esteem.

Goals can be long-term and substantial, such as completing a degree or renovating a house. You can also set short-term goals, such as arriving at the decision to finally throw out all the junk that you have been tripping over in your shed for the past year. If you have a history of starting projects that you rarely finish, plan your activity from start to finish. Make a list of the actions required to complete the task and tick them off as they are achieved.

9. Stop judging yourself harshly

In the chapter on anxiety, depression and stress we discuss how punishing ourselves with the tyranny of the 'shoulds' and 'musts' can affect our emotional wellbeing. Part of accepting yourself includes replacing expressions such as 'I should do . . .' with 'I would like to do . . .' or 'It would be *better* if I did such and such . . . but not *essential*.'

10. Mix with people who are positive

If you regularly associate with people who have a persistently negative attitude to life, you will need extraordinary strengths to resist being dragged down by them. This does not mean that you should abandon friends or relatives who are experiencing personal problems. However, if you are the type of caring person who seems to attract troubled people in their droves, make a conscious decision to limit the time you spend with them. You will be amazed at the effect of reducing time with negative people, and replacing it with time with those for whom life is positive and exciting.

11. Replace negative self-talk with positive self-talk

Next time you are about to say or think something negative about someone – stop! Look for one of their better points. For example, replace 'Jane is staid and boring' with, 'Over the years Jane has proven herself to be a loyal and caring friend'. Of course, your replacement statement does need to be true!

12. Write a daily affirmation

At the end of each day, write down one point that makes you feel good about yourself. It could be a goal that you met, kindness that you extended to another person, or simply completing a particular project.

After you have made your daily list, keep it and add to it. This version of the 'shoebox' will help you feel good about yourself when you find that your self-esteem is taking a battering.

SUMMARY:

In this chapter we . . .

- Discussed some of the behaviours of people with low self-esteem.
- Discovered the relationship between self-esteem and our self-concept.
- Examined how our self-concept is shaped.
- Looked at the ways in which retirement can impact on our self-esteem.
- Discovered ways of improving and maintaining our levels of self-esteem as adults.

CHECKLIST

- ☐ I understand the difference between 'self-concept' and 'self-esteem'.
- ☐ I have challenged destructive messages from the 'voices from the past'.
- ☐ I have started my own 'shoebox' of positive feedback.
- ☐ I have studied the twelve ideas for building my self-esteem and have put a number of them into practice.

CHAPTER NINE

Understanding grief and loss

AIMS OF THIS CHAPTER

- To understand the effects of grief and loss.
- To examine ways to help ourselves during times of grief.
- To examine ways of helping others who are grieving.

Note: In this book, there have been frequent references to the effect of retirement lifestyle issues on relationships. It is important to devote time to relationship issues because in retirement people in relationships tend to spend much more time together. However, I have always been conscious of the many people reading this book who either do not have a partner, or who have lost their partner due to death or separation. Where such frequent references to partners are a source of further pain to those living alone, I am truly sorry. I hope the following chapter goes some way to helping you gain more of the happiness you deserve in retirement.

What is grief?

Grief consists of our physical, psychological and social responses to the loss of someone we love, or to whom we are closely bonded in friendship. While most people associate grief with the death of a person, the symptoms of grief may also arise due to the loss of our job at retirement, through the loss of a friendship, or through divorce.

Because the range of emotions associated with grieving is so diverse and intense, those experiencing grief may sometimes wonder if they are going crazy. Yet despite these feelings, grief is a very normal response to the tragedy of personal loss. In fact, psychologists who specialise in the area of grief counselling are far more likely to be concerned by a lack of demonstrable grief in a recently bereaved person than by the healthy process of grieving.

For how long do people grieve?

Over the years there have been a number of popular books published that describe the 'stages' of grief those in mourning experience. It has sometimes been easy to gain the impression from these books that grief is a predictable, orderly process whereby the mourner begins at one end, proceeds through a number of predictable stages, and emerges 'cured' out the other end. However, as people who have experienced grief will tell you, the process of grieving rarely, if ever, has any bearing on logic. Each individual who experiences grief does so in their own way and in their own time.

However, while grief is very much an individual response to loss, there are usually a number of processes that those in mourning share.

1. Shock

Where death has occurred suddenly, those who were close to the deceased will naturally experience shock. An unexpected fatal heart attack or accidental death catapults the deceased's loved ones into instant trauma. However, shock can still occur even when death is expected following a long illness. This occurs because those involved in caring for their loved one have typically been in a state of heightened anxiety and stress during the illness. Consequently, they have not had the time nor the emotional space to prepare themselves for their loved one's death.

To complicate matters further, there is often the desperate hope that a cure will be found, or that the patient will live longer than the medical profession is predicting. These hopes and anxieties can create a high level of denial so that when death does eventually occur, the shock is almost as severe as that experienced from a sudden death.

One symptom of the trauma in such circumstances is psychological or emotional numbness. Many people describe that immediately after the death of a loved one, their day-to-day life resembles a dreamlike state in which they experience feelings of being detached from reality. These feelings can go on for some days and it is common during these times to feel like a spectator looking on as the rest of the world goes by. Life may seem to consist of a series of actions occurring on 'automatic pilot' and conscious decision-making is absent. Such emotional turmoil can be very frightening, and has people beginning to question their own sanity.

2. Denial

Denial can occur on a number of levels. The dying person and the loved ones will often remain in a state of denial regarding the terminal nature of the condition. A typical response is, 'This can't be happening to us!' or, 'There must be some mistake – maybe the test results were for someone else.' In the case of divorce or separation, denial may take the form of, 'Perhaps they will come back to me soon' or 'When they have got this temporary fling out of their system they will come running back'.

Remaining in denial has a number of negative side effects. For example, the person who is dying may never have the opportunity to organise their affairs and, therefore, important matters such as making a will, or arranging a power of attorney, may be left until it is too late. This can cause financial and emotional difficulties for those surviving at the very time when they need as few worries as possible.

When a person is in denial over a relationship that has ended, they continue to place themselves in a stressful no-man's land by putting off the day when they deal with their grief.

3. Psychological, physiological and social responses

Physical responses to grief include our increased vulnerability to stress-related illnesses, while psychological responses include anxiety and depression. At a social level, responses include the ways in which we find ourselves interacting with our friends and family.

From the mourner's perspective, psychological and social responses to grief can be compounded by the observation that while their own world seems to have ended, others around them soon return to their normal routines of work and family life. Looking on as friends and relatives appear to function, unscathed by the loss, often adds to the overwhelming sense of emptiness that many mourners feel.

Along with feelings of psychological isolation can come a range of other unwanted psychological effects. Some people describe feeling that they are becoming more like the deceased in a number of ways, and that aspects of the deceased's personality or repertoire of behaviours are being incorporated into their own personal make-up. At the same time, physical problems such as loss of appetite and sleep disturbances can emerge just as the grieving person is at their most vulnerable.

4. Guilt

Feelings of guilt invariably surface during the grieving process. Those close to the deceased may start to regret the way in which they had handled past disputes, or may regret that they had not done more for the deceased. They may also find themselves regretting that they had not been more open about the way in which they expressed love and affection for their loved one. Such guilt is usually misplaced and fails to take into account the personalities of the deceased and of those around them. For example, for some people hugging and public statements such as 'I love you' are difficult or embarrassing, although they may seem like missed opportunities once the person has died.

5. Anger

Grieving relatives will often find themselves experiencing feelings of anger that, paradoxically, are directed towards the deceased: 'They had no right to leave me alone like this!' While this is a very common grieving response, it can also be a bewildering experience. However, it is normal during such times and, like many of the other responses to grief, does not mean that the person is 'going mad', despite what they may be tempted to believe.

The person who is dying may also feel anger that they direct towards the medical profession for not having diagnosed the complaint earlier or treated the illness more successfully. Anger may also result from the dying person's frustration that their long-term plans will now not be completed.

6. The 'pedestal' effect

At some stage early in the grieving process, people usually find themselves focusing on the good aspects of the deceased while ignoring, or even denying, their less pleasant sides. Sometimes when listening to grieving people reminisce, it could be assumed that the deceased was a saint! However, after experiencing so much pain and shock, those left grieving are in desperate need of fond memories to reinforce the positive aspects of their relationship with the deceased.

7. Reality

During this stage, the bereaved will start to regain their view of the deceased person as a normal human being who had good and less favourable aspects to their make-up. It is during this time that the accuracy of statements such as, 'If only they were still alive I would never complain again!' are questioned as the bereaved puts a more realistic interpretation on their relationship with their late friend or partner.

8. Acceptance, adjustment and growth

These final grief processes occur when the bereaved finally accepts their loss and acknowledges the need to move on as an individual. Where partnerships have been close knit, with most activities and social occasions carried out as a couple, the surviving partner may find that their first steps out into the world again are simultaneously daunting and exciting. It is during this time that fine-tuning communication skills and the ability to manage anxiety become important (see the chapters on communication and on anxiety, depression and stress).

Managing grief and loss

Support groups – a helping hand when you need it

Sometimes well-meaning people will say to a grieving friend or relative, 'I know how you feel.' They then may be surprised to hear the grieving person angrily snap back with, 'How could you know how I feel?' In fact, the grieving person is correct! How could anyone else know how they feel if they have not experienced the circumstances the grieving person is going through? It is because of the need for people in mourning to share their grief with those who really understand that self-help groups such as SOLACE have formed. To attend SOLACE meetings people must have lost their partner due to death. The thinking behind such self-help groups is that the only people who really know how others feel during grief are those who have experienced the same type of pain and loss.

Because each person grieves differently, self-help groups like SOLACE benefit some people more than others. People also differ regarding the timing of their attendance at self-help groups. For example, some people find themselves benefiting from self-help groups a couple of weeks after their partner's death, while others may wait months or years. Whatever the case, the important point to remember is that these self-help groups are designed to provide those who are grieving with a safe, supportive environment where they can share the burden of their pain and loneliness with others. Consequently, the level of participation at self-help groups is voluntary, so that if an attendee just feels like sitting and listening while others discuss their own grief, it is okay to do so.

There are many different kinds of self-help groups that have been formed to help people grieve about their particular type of loss. If you are grieving, and feel that you could benefit from attending a self-help group, contact your local library or municipal office for a list of the self-help groups in your area.

Rebound relationships

'My husband and I had been close friends with the couple across the road for over thirty years – our children even went to the same school. When my husband died a year after my neighbour's wife, we started going out, just for company. We married soon after because I thought I knew him so well. It wasn't until after our wedding that I discovered my mistake!'

Unfortunately, by the time people retire some have already lost their partner due to death. It is around our fifties and sixties that we begin to see an elevated incidence of death and terminal illness among our friends and family. In fact, a number of those participating in the *Retire 200* research retired early to care for an ill partner or family member. Sometimes these carers were eventually faced with the death of the person they were caring for and then found themselves dealing simultaneously with the joint issues of grief and adjustment to retirement.

It is during times such as these, when people are lonely and emotionally raw, that the decision to enter a new relationship may be made for the wrong reasons. The initial relief from loneliness may only be short lived if the relationship is not founded on the important components of mutual trust and respect, commonality of interests, and all the other variables that make a relationship work.

Helping a friend or relative who is grieving

Because the death of someone close is such a traumatic experience, friends or relatives of the bereaved may desperately want to help but feel that they do not know what they should do. Usually this reluctance is based either on their own discomfort, or the concern that if they do or say the wrong thing they will only make matters worse. However, what people really need when they are grieving is the company and support of those they are closest to. The very worst thing that people can do is to stay away from them when they need support most.

Of course, when you are helping people whose emotions are fragile, it is wise to be prepared for their emotional responses to be quite different to the responses you have been used to during less stressful times. For example, some years ago a friend of mine (then in his teens), visited the home of a friend whose father had died the previous day. Without thinking, he greeted his friend's mother with, 'How are things?' It was the type of automatic friendly greeting he usually gave her and he had clearly not thought through the type of reaction such a greeting could receive at this time. He was therefore horrified when she snapped back with an icy, 'Under the circumstances I think that is a most inappropriate question!' as she stormed out of the room.

Naturally everyone is different and will bring their own personality to the experience of grief. However, the following list of general dos and don'ts may help if you are assisting someone through the crisis of grief.

What to do

- If they wish to cry and to share their grief, let them do so. Do not try to stop them because *you* feel uncomfortable. It is a good emotional release for them and is part of a healthy grieving process.
- Tell them you are sorry for what has happened. Do not be afraid to say this in case you make them cry.
- Be available to listen to them and to help them with anything that seems to need doing.
- Encourage them to keep talking if they want to discuss their loved one.
- Encourage them to take sufficient time to get over the shock caused by the death of their friend or loved one. Many people will say things like, 'I should be getting over this by now', when in fact only a few weeks or months have passed.

What not to do

- Do not try to rush the grieving process by implying that the grieving person needs to put grief behind them as soon as possible.
- Do not tell them you 'know how they feel' unless you have been through a similar experience yourself. Even where you have suffered a similar loss, the grieving person may feel that their own grief is more severe due to the special relationship they felt they had with their friend or partner.
- Do not avoid those in mourning because you feel you do not have anything to offer them. Your company and concern will be invaluable to them. If they genuinely wish to be left alone at times, you should of course respect that too.
- Do not try to change the subject when they want to discuss their loved one. People will sometimes do this in the genuine belief that they are saving the grieving person from unnecessarily

upsetting themselves. However, the process of talking about their loved one is important at this time.

- Do not avoid using the deceased's name for fear of upsetting the person in mourning.
- Do not attempt to look for positive aspects of the deceased's death. For the bereaved person the death was a tragedy and this view needs to be respected.

SUMMARY:

In this chapter we . . .

- Identified the ways in which emotions and wellbeing are affected when people grieve.
- Examined ways of helping those close to us who may be grieving.

CHECKLIST

- ☐ I understand why self-help groups are especially relevant during times of grief.
- ☐ I understand the processes that we go through when we are grieving.
- ☐ I understand that grieving is a healthy, necessary process.
- ☐ I now know how to help those around me who are grieving.

CHAPTER TEN

Ending loneliness

AIMS OF THIS CHAPTER

- To examine the effects of loneliness.
- To examine how we form friendships and bond with others.
- To identify methods of combating loneliness.

Loneliness

People say that you can be lonely even when you are in a crowd. A number of those on the *Retire 200* program had divorced or separated from unhappy marriages. Many commented that they had not realised how lonely they had been in their dysfunctional relationships until after their partnership had dissolved. Living with someone who is either perpetually morose or non-communicative can result in feelings of anxiety or depression similar to those experienced when loneliness is due to isolation.

Loneliness versus anxiety or depression

There is a growing body of evidence to suggest that many diagnoses of anxiety and depression are predicated on the real underlying problem of loneliness. Some years ago, a study of stress among dentists concluded that many of them were suffering from the effects of 'professional isolation', or loneliness. The initial theory had suggested that the probable cause of dentists' stress levels was their constant association with anxious patients. However, it was eventually found that stress for this group of dentists was related to the fact that their 'best' work was not witnessed by their professional peers. At the end of the day all the patient wanted was their teeth fixed with a minimum of pain; the fact that this feat was achieved through applying a technically difficult procedure was of little interest to them.

So how is the dilemma of dentists' stress relevant to those of us who are lonely? Essentially the issues are similar in that successes or achievements may go largely unrecognised and reinforced when we are alone. If we paint a room in the house, or prepare an attractive garden bed, the satisfaction gained may not seem quite the same if there is no one there to admire our achievements.

The psychological symptoms of loneliness

Loneliness occurs when people feel there is nobody with whom they can communicate intimately and openly on a regular basis. Lonely people report feeling bored, sad, nervous, worthless, powerless, or absorbed with their own sense of emotional isolation. This problem is compounded because society reinforces the worth of people in relationships. It is, therefore, easy for those who are lonely to feel excluded from the mainstream of life. The subsequent feelings of isolation may then affect self-esteem and lead to feelings of hopelessness.

A common paradox occurs when lonely people become overly critical of others, blaming them for not making sufficient effort to rescue them from their loneliness. Consequently, some lonely people reject the well-intentioned approaches of others as not 'good enough'. If they persist in rejecting enough people for long enough, lonely people can set up a self-fulfilling prophecy that says, 'Because people don't really care that I am lonely, and will not make sufficient effort to help me, I do not wish to interact with them.'

Such people may continue to remain lonely because of the impossibly high expectations they have about what constitutes friendship. Their demanding criteria may include:

- 'True friends are always available.'
- 'True friends always agree with my political, religious, and social values.'

These criteria set up some lonely people for disappointment as new friendships dissolve when unrealistic expectations fail to be realised.

Understanding why we like others and why they like us

Knowing what it is that attracts us to others, and them to us, can be helpful when we are feeling wary about socialising again after a long period of loneliness. It is quite natural for our self-esteem to be a little ragged at this time; taking some of the mystery out of the bonding processes in friendship can give us the confidence we need to get started.

1. Geographical location

FAMILIARITY

The more familiar a person is to us, the more we find that we want to interact with them. Most people prefer to chat to people they know than to a stranger.

AVAILABILITY

The nearer people live to each other, the higher the probability of them forming a relationship that may end up as a friendship. Studies of people living in large blocks of units have even shown that people form friendships more readily with their immediate neighbours than with residents living just a few units away.

PREDICTABILITY

The better we know someone, the more likely we are to be able to predict how they will react in specific situations. This allows us to avoid accidentally annoying them with comments that may be in direct conflict with their beliefs. They too learn that we find certain behaviours annoying or offensive, and have the opportunity to avoid them as they build a friendship with us.

INTERACTION

Interacting with others on a regular basis increases the likelihood of us forming a relationship with them. Social research indicates that where we have regular interactions with a person, we will look for evidence to convince ourselves that they are interesting, intelligent, or special in some way.

2. Physical/personal attributes

PHYSICAL ATTRACTIVENESS

It seems that attractive people do have an easier time making friends, particularly during the early stages of friendship. However, if, like most of us, you are not a raving beauty, do not despair! Social research provides us with two reassuring facts:

- Studies of couples in long-term relationships indicate that people usually pair up with those who are about equal to them on perceived attractiveness.
- For relationships to endure, other aspects of the relationship such as commonality of interests, general politeness and pleasantness are more important than good looks.

WARMTH

People like to be around those who have a warm personality. From a psychological perspective, 'warmth' relates to the tendency of people to rate other people and events positively rather than negatively. It also includes being accepting of others rather than being aloof or overcritical. Accordingly, those who usually see the positive aspects of people are more appealing to us than those whose typical attitude is to find fault.

Apart from the congenial atmosphere surrounding warm people, their general air of approval encourages those around them to self-disclose in a safe environment. This is an important personal attribute because being able to safely self-disclose is one of the key risk-taking behaviours intrinsic to the relationships of close friends.

THE HALO EFFECT

The halo effect describes our tendency to rate people highly if we find them attractive, or gifted in one particular area. For example, a person who loves classical music may highly rate the overall worth of a person who is an authority on music, although they may have a number of unpleasant aspects to their personality. Similarly, the halo effect operates where a neat, well-dressed person is regarded as more intelligent or more capable than their untidy, overweight colleague even though there is no factual basis for this assessment.

The relevance of the halo effect to making new friends is simply that we tend to bond most easily with those who we see as competent in areas we regard as important. Once we identify an aspect of a new acquaintance's make-up or values that aligns closely with our own, we are more likely to regard them favourably. One participant of the *Retire 200* program told of moving into a new neighbourhood shortly after retiring. His next-door neighbour was fastidious in the way he maintained his garden and came over to introduce himself simply because the new arrival mowed the lawn the day after moving in!

COMMONALITY

Given the choice, people prefer to be in the company of those with similar attitudes to their own. When we are with people who see life the way we do, our own values are reinforced and we feel good about ourselves. Consequently, people of a particular culture, religion, or sporting interest will find that they are more comfortable in the company of others with similar preferences or views.

Ways to manage loneliness

Strategies for dealing with loneliness

No one strategy for dealing with loneliness will suit all people. Each of us varies in the way we socialise, in our levels of self-confidence, and in the types of activities we find enjoyable. If loneliness is an ongoing problem for you, assess how you are performing in the following areas:

1. Your attitudes
2. Your skills
3. Your behaviours.

Let's look at these three areas now – in particular, we will examine the aspects of behaviours that can help smooth the way for you as you start to form new friendships.

1. Your attitudes

Ask yourself the following questions and try to answer them as honestly as you can. Where you detect some attitudes that can be improved, put some work into them.

AM I EQUATING 'BEING ALONE' WITH LONELINESS?

We all need some time alone to read books, to think about life and to plan. In fact, not having enough time alone can be a major source of stress. It is only when we find that we are alone too often for our own liking that we become lonely.

DO I SET UNREALISTICALLY HIGH CRITERIA FOR HOW I EXPECT MY FAMILY AND FRIENDS TO BEHAVE TOWARDS ME?

Am I demanding that family and friends are always there for me regardless of their own needs and schedules? Do I define loyalty and friendship in black-and-white terms where people 'must' behave according to my standards at all times?

If we set unrealistically high standards for other people's behaviour, we are heading for disappointment. It is rare indeed to find a friend whose values will always be the same as ours in every aspect of life. For example, I have a friend who I know would be there for me under any circumstances. I have another friend who makes me laugh more than anyone I know, yet in a time of need would probably run in the opposite direction. Our friendship is based not on dependability or loyalty but, rather, on our keen mutual sense of the ridiculous.

DO I BLAME OTHERS FOR MY UNHAPPINESS?

For example, when an acquaintance stops making contact as regularly as they used to, it may just be that the relationship has run its course or that there are no longer sufficient areas of mutual interest to keep it alive. It also can be that their own lives are full and that they are flat out dealing with their responsibilities. When this occurs it is usually no one person's fault and you do not need to attribute blame to yourself or to them.

AM I BECOMING SELF-CENTRED?

It is very easy for lonely people to spend too much time dwelling on their own predicament. Apart from causing themselves unnecessary anxiety and depression, they can become painfully self-centred, which exacerbates their problems in finding new social contacts.

When you start meeting people after a period of loneliness, try to avoid the temptation to pour out all of the worries and concerns that you have been storing up. Listening to the problems of established friends is one thing; having to listen to those of a new acquaintance will usually send people scurrying for cover.

2. Your skills

DO I LACK THE NECESSARY SOCIAL SKILLS WHEN FORMING NEW RELATIONSHIPS?

Facing new social situations can be daunting for some people even when all is going well in their lives. Where loneliness has been a persistent problem, it may signal that assertiveness skills require practice so that the difficult first steps can be taken to establish social contacts. Chapter Three provides some strategies if using assertive behaviour is a problem for you.

DO I COMMUNICATE EFFECTIVELY WITH OTHERS?

An excellent way to start relating with someone that you have just met is to quickly demonstrate to them that you are a good listener. Chapter Two provides specific ways of improving interpersonal communication skills – for now, however, the following points may be helpful.

- When first meeting someone that you are interested in getting to know better, make a determined effort to listen closely to them.
- Demonstrate that you are listening by periodically feeding back the content of what they have said, and asking questions. For example:

They say:	'I bought a computer recently to keep track of my stamp collection, complete my tax returns . . . you know, that sort of thing.'
Your response:	'A computer! How do you use the computer to complete your tax returns?'

By following up with a question, we demonstrate that we have been tuned in to what they are saying. We are then more likely to hold their interest than if we tried to impress them by talking about ourselves.

3. Your behaviours

Overcoming loneliness takes determination and action. People will not usually beat a path to your door to rescue you from your plight, so it is up to you to start the ball rolling. Here are some steps you can take to begin combating loneliness.

MAKE A LIST OF NEW PLACES TO GO

If you go to new places, you are more likely to meet new people. The range of places you can go to meet people is virtually limitless. You can join clubs, enrol in courses, go to free concerts in parks, attend art exhibitions, flower shows . . . anywhere you have the opportunity to start a casual conversation with people in a safe, friendly environment.

Another benefit associated with moving out of your usual territory is that it is much easier to approach strangers when you are not in your own neighbourhood. For example, people who would normally find it difficult to approach strangers will do so with comparative ease when asking for directions in a strange city. Having a legitimate 'excuse' to speak with others removes a lot of the self-consciousness we may be feeling.

OPEN A CONVERSATION

As you mingle at functions, look around the group for people you think you may like. Open a casual conversation with them about something relevant to the occasion. For example: 'That's a beautiful painting, isn't it?' or, 'Have you been on one of these courses before?'

Of course, not all of the people you approach will wish to chat. They may have come there to relax, or may be so absorbed by the event that they will wish to focus their attention on it. It is important that you understand their needs and that you try not to interpret their reluctance to talk as a personal rejection. At times, you may find that the ratio of initial approaches to ongoing conversations is quite low. However, in the meantime you are already achieving the following:

- You have pushed your loneliness to one side as you courageously empower yourself by mixing with other people.
- Each approach brings you one step closer to meeting someone with whom you can form a friendship or spend some time.

MANAGING ANXIETY

When you enter a new social environment, it is easy to interpret the anticipation you are feeling as anxiety. Paradoxically, the symptoms of anxiety can be much the same as the feelings we get when we are anticipating something pleasant. For example, on the morning of leaving for a long-awaited overseas holiday, people may awaken with butterflies in the stomach, an elevated pulse rate, and sweaty palms. Yet these are the same symptoms that we experience during an attack of anxiety. It is, therefore, important to remind yourself that if you experience such feelings in new social situations, it is quite normal.

If you find that anxiety does become a problem during your encounters, refer to Chapter Seven on anxiety, depression and stress, where you may find some techniques to help you relax.

TAKING THE INITIAL CONVERSATION A STEP FURTHER

After talking for a while with a new person, you may wish to take the relationship to the next level by suggesting a further meeting. Gauge the situation before deciding how you are going to take the next steps. For example, if you are a man and the other person is a woman, it would be wise to suggest meeting for a cup of coffee or lunch somewhere on neutral, public territory, such as a restaurant or coffee shop. The important thing to remember is that the other person needs to feel safe and to feel that they can 'escape' easily if things do not go well.

Ending loneliness

Help other lonely people

When we are lonely, it is easy for us to focus on our own dilemmas, which usually does little to improve our situation. Consider providing company and assistance to other lonely people. By focusing on others, you will find that you begin to forget your own problems – and there is certainly no shortage of people who need help. If this idea appeals to you, try contacting a few charities and offering your services.

Stay involved

Happy people are rarely idle – they stay involved and are usually prepared to try new ideas. Try doing something you have never done before, just for the fun of it. For example, if there is a subject you hold strong views about, write a few letters to the papers about it and see if they are published.

Escapism – taking the easy way out

When we are lonely or depressed we may find ourselves spending a lot of time sleeping. The problem with this is that too much sleep can just be an escape from problems or miseries that are still there when we wake up. Moreover, spending too much time in bed can be physically detrimental as muscles atrophy, resulting in weakness. One answer to this problem is to set a schedule of rising at the same time each day as if you were going to work. This technique was used successfully by several of the participants on the *Retire 200* program. Also make sure that you schedule tasks for yourself during the day and avoid other escapes such as watching too much television or abusing alcohol or drugs.

Stay involved with your community

Find ways of connecting with the rest of your community. If you find the prospect of joining community organisations a little daunting, try starting by just attending as an interested observer. Council meetings and lobby groups are a good place to start, as they usually welcome observers.

Join a club or group

Check with your local council or the Yellow Pages or go online to compile a list of groups or clubs to join. You will be surprised at the range of activities that are available. Even if none of these appeals to you, the process of looking may help you generate other ideas for activities such as short courses at the local U3A (University of the Third Age).

Moving from planning to action

You may have read the preceding pages and felt that there were some ideas that you could put into action. If you did, you are off to a great start. However, if you have been lonely for some time, or if your loneliness has resulted from the end of a long relationship or marriage, you may find that you require some motivation to get going. A good way to achieve momentum in such situations is to draw up an action plan of goals.

Action plans do not have to be elaborate. In fact, the clearer and easier they are to write and maintain, the more likely you are to actually use them! Here is an action plan that you can use to ensure that you maximise the likelihood of meeting new friends or acquaintances. You may wish to use it as it is, or (preferably) adapt it to meet your own needs and circumstances.

Sunday evening

Go through the weekend papers and the local weekly paper to search for advertisements, notices or articles about free or interesting events such as art shows, concerts, openings and book readings.

Every day

Keep a notebook or sheet of paper in your purse or wallet and write down the details of coming events that you see advertised in your daily travels to the shops or elsewhere.

Set up a planner

Use a diary, or wall calendar, or a computer-based calendar such as that found in Microsoft Outlook in which to record the times and venues of all the events you have found in your search. Fill your week with as many potential events as possible.

Act!

Up until now, it has been an academic exercise. Now is the time for action. Decide which of the events you are going to attend and make sure you go. Be courageous – do not put it off! DO IT!

SUMMARY:

In this chapter we . . .

- Differentiated loneliness from anxiety and depression.
- Examined how and why we affiliate with other people.
- Listed attitudes, skills and behaviours associated with successful affiliation.
- Designed an action plan to end loneliness.

CHECKLIST

- ☐ I have examined the list of attitudes, skills and behaviours required to form new friendships and will take action to improve my social skills where this is necessary.
- ☐ I have designed my own action plan to ensure that I attend sufficient social occasions each week.

SECTION FOUR

The impact of personality and the need to cross-skill

Gaining insight into how our personality and the personalities of our partner and friends affect our lives can be a valuable experience. People who explore why they react the way they do in certain situations often describe a profound sense of relief at what they discover. They may learn, for example, that their own lack of success in a particular area is not because they are dumb or lazy. Rather, it is because the area concerned is not one where they naturally prefer to focus their attention. Similarly, people in relationships discover why it is that their partner reacts differently from themselves in some situations and not others. Such insight can remove a sense of irritation that might have been present in the relationship for years.

In the second chapter in this section of the book, we examine the need for partners to cross-skill so that both individuals can perform all roles and responsibilities presently shared between them.

CHAPTER ELEVEN

How personality preferences affect your life in retirement

AIM OF THIS CHAPTER

- To learn how our personality and the personalities of others may impact on our adjustment to life in retirement.

Note: Not everyone arrives at retirement with a partner. However, personality affects more than just the interactions of those in a relationship. Gaining insight into your personality style can help explain why it is that, in certain situations, you seem to feel ill at ease or to experience stress and discomfort. Just as important is understanding why you excel in other situations, so that you can capitalise on them. Similarly, having a basic understanding of the structure of personality can help you understand why others around you react to situations in the way that they do.

What is personality?

In the following chapter, we will look at some aspects of personality developed back in the early twentieth century by Carl Jung, a Swiss psychiatrist. Much of Jung's work is viewed by today's psychologists as somewhat fanciful and lacking in the ability to be tested scientifically. However, a number of his views on personality have endured and form the basis of personality inventories such as the *Keirsey Temperament Scale* and the *Myer-Briggs Type Indicator* (MBTI).

The areas we will examine comprise four sets of personality preferences, namely:

1. Introversion (I) versus Extraversion (E)
2. Sensing (S) versus Intuition (N)
3. Feeling (F) versus Thinking (T)
4. Fixed Schedule (FS) versus (PS) Planned Schedule.

As you read the descriptions of each pair of opposite personality preferences, you may find that you identify more with one preference of each pair than with its opposite. This is by no means a foolproof method of identifying your personality preferences but may serve to provide you with some insight into where they may lie.

Personality and relationships

The effects of personality on your relationship with your partner

The old saying 'opposites attract' appears to be true when it comes to the choice of our partner. While opposites may attract in the early stages of a relationship, the daily process of effectively interacting with each other in a stress-free manner is made more difficult where significant personality differences are present. However, if both people in a relationship understand *why* they each prefer to act as they do, it can go a long way to reducing stress. This can be particularly important during retirement when you and your partner are going to be spending more time together than when you were working.

Some aspects of personality explained

1. Extraversion (E) versus Introversion (I)

Ask ten psychologists to define Extraversion and Introversion and you may come away confused as you attempt to process ten different views. For our purposes, however, we will define Extraversion as a focus on the outer world of people and things, and Introversion as a focus on the inner world of concepts and ideas. The following table illustrates some of the differences between Extraverts and Introverts. As you read it, ask yourself which one of the two columns best describes your preferences.

Extraversion (E)	Introversion (I)
Breadth, action and variety	Depth, quiet concentration
May prefer mixing with a wide range of people	May prefer the close friendship of a few people than mixing with a wide range of people
May put social life before private life	Value their private life before their social life
May prefer to join in the hurly-burly of a group discussion than to speak quietly with one person	May prefer to speak quietly with one person than to join in the hurly-burly of a group discussion
People, things	Ideas, quiet thinking
Prefer action and change and may act on the spur of the moment	Do not mind focusing on the one task for considerable periods of time
Prefer to work with a lot of other people around	Prefer to work with fewer people around
Sometimes act before they think	More likely to think first then act
Would rather discuss a topic with someone than quietly reflect on it	Think before taking action and tend to reflect on ideas before discussing them with others

In today's society you often find that people have gained the incorrect perception that being Extraverted is in some way better than being Introverted. For example, you may hear people saying something like, 'Fred is a fantastic bloke – he's a real Extravert!' Extraverted behaviour is highly desirable in some circumstances, for example, if approaching strangers to request donations for your favourite charity. However, Introverted behaviour is highly desirable in others, for example, spending several quiet hours bringing the financial records of your social club up to date. This is not to suggest that the Introvert is incapable of approaching strangers for donations, or that the Extravert could not focus on the lonely job of working on the club's records. It is just that Extraverts tend to *prefer* tasks involving interaction with people, and Introverts will often *prefer* tasks where they can quietly focus.

Below are examples of the differing behaviours that were needed to write this book:

Introverting behaviours (I)	Extraverting behaviours (E)
• Design methodology for the research program in which the retirement experiences of 200 retirees were examined (50+ hours) • Collate and process the data of 200 retirees (300+ hours) • Statistically analyse data and draw conclusions (60+ hours) • Write research paper (800+ hours) • Write the book (2,000+ hours)	• Discuss research design with university staff (12+ hours) • Interview 200 retirees (200+ hours) • Discuss the proposed book with the publisher (3+ hours) • Speak at publisher's marketing meeting (1+ hours) • Attend book launch (2 hours)
Total Introverting hours = 3,210+	Total Extraverting hours = 218+

2. How we see the world around us – Sensing (S) versus Intuition (N)

Those with the Sensing preference (S) are sometimes described as living in the 'here and now', using their five senses to take in information accurately – for example, seeing the Sydney Harbour Bridge as an excellent piece of engineering. Those with the Intuitive preference (N) may prefer to put a more global interpretation on what they see and even look for the symbolic picture – for example, seeing the Sydney Harbour Bridge as a metaphor for Australia.

Sensing (S)	Intuition (N)
Are often more interested in measurable and tangible facts than in abstract theories and possibilities	Are often more interested in abstract theories and possibilities than in measurable and tangible facts

Sensing (S)	**Intuition (N)**
Believe it is better to apply existing processes based on experience than to try theories and predictions of what could be	Believe theories and predictions of what could be are more interesting than using existing processes based on experience
Common sense	Imagination
Decisions may be based on experience	Decisions may be based on a hunch
Described as practical and down to earth rather than as dreamers of new ideas or concepts	Described as dreamers of new ideas or concepts rather than as practical and down to earth
Fine detail – accuracy	Overview – big picture
Have a good eye for detail and are good at picking flaws in a design, or the fine detail in a piece of art	View the world in a global way but may fail to see detail such as an important or incorrect number buried in a detailed profit and loss statement
Now, facts, reality	Future, possibility, dreams
Often regarded as more predictable than innovative	Often regarded as more innovative than predictable
May be seen more as realistic than imaginative	May be seen more as imaginative than realistic

Those with a Sensing preference are more likely to rely on past experience as their most highly valued basis for arriving at decisions. Intuitives, on the other hand, tend to look more for what possibilities the future holds for them. Consequently, while those who are Sensing are sometimes described as realistic, or 'grounded', and living in the real world, Intuitives are more likely to look forward to change and to events in the future.

3. How we arrive at decisions – Thinking (T) versus Feeling (F)

The labels 'Thinking' and 'Feeling' do not mean to imply that those with a Feeling preference do not think, or that those with a Thinking preference are incapable of feeling! Rather, the labels indicate that *when it comes to making decisions*, people with the Thinking preference are more likely to rely on objective logic and will be influenced mostly by facts. Those with the Feeling preference may prefer to make decisions where the outcomes are less likely to affect other people adversely.

It should also be emphasised that both those with the Feeling preference and those with the Thinking preference can react with similar levels of emotional intensity. It is simply that those with the Feeling preference tend to display their emotions more openly. Sometimes such open displays can be a problem for any Ts who happen to be around at the time. They may find themselves becoming embarrassed by what they see as inappropriate or excessive displays of emotion.

Thinking (T)	**Feeling (F)**
Are described more often as rational than obeying their heart when making decisions	Are seen as more often obeying their heart than their head when making decisions
Are more likely to be seen as firm and decisive rather than compassionate	Are more likely to be seen as warm and compassionate rather than firm and decisive
Are more likely to be seen as logical and clear thinking than as concerned about others' feelings	Are more likely to be seen as concerned about other's feelings than as logical or objective
Intellect, justice	Emotion, humanity
Look for facts that are clear and measurable to build their case when arguing a point	Tend to use persuasion rather than logic when trying to win an argument
Prefer to identify what has gone wrong than to provide sympathy and comfort	Prefer to provide sympathy and comfort than to identify what has gone wrong

Thinking (T)	Feeling (F)
Tend to rely on logic and objectivity when making decisions	Are more likely to make decisions based on the impact they will have on other people
When they see situations where people are not performing well at a task, they find it comparatively easy to tell them where they are going wrong	When they see situations where people are not performing well at a task, they may find it difficult to tell them where they are going wrong

4. How and when we act on our decisions – Planned Schedule (PS) preference versus Flexible Schedule (FS) preference

Those with the Planned Schedule (PS) preference are keen to act on decisions according to plan and have what some people have described as a 'high need for closure'. Those with the Flexible Schedule (FS) preference, on the other hand, may feel pressured by a tight deadline, arguing that they need time to gather more information before they act, just in case there is some important issue that has not yet been considered.

Flexible Schedule (FS)	Planned Schedule (PS)
Are more comfortable with change and spontaneity	Are more comfortable with a routine that is predictable
Even if they are working to an agreed plan or schedule, changes along the way make the otherwise predictable routine more interesting	If they are working to an agreed plan or schedule, they dislike changes along the way
Having daily plans to stick to restricts them too much	Not knowing what their plans are makes them uneasy until they have a plan in place
Keep options open	Work to plan
Let life happen, adapt, keep exploring	Manage life, plan, decide

Flexible Schedule (FS)	Planned Schedule (PS)
Prefer to keep options open	Wish to get things completed as soon as possible
Spontaneous, play, adventure	Controlled, work, order
Tend to get very enthusiastic at the start of projects but become bored when it comes to putting on the finishing touches	Tend to work steadily during projects from start to finish
When a decision has been made they may become restless and worry that they should have obtained more information before making the decision	Take deadlines very seriously and will be disappointed if others do not do likewise
Would rather let life unfold than stick to predictable schedules or plans	Would rather stick to predictable schedules or plans than just to let life unfold

How to apply knowledge of personality preferences to your life in retirement

Your personality and life in retirement

In this section, we will look at how aspects of personality affect our life in retirement.

If you are an Extravert (E)

- You will need to ensure that you are involved in a sufficiently wide range of activities to provide you with variety. This is important if you are to remain challenged and stimulated.

- You will need to ensure that your activities allow sufficient opportunities to interact with groups of people rather than just comprising quiet, solitary tasks.
- Extraverts are known for their tendency to act quickly, sometimes without thinking matters through carefully enough. While this can make Extraverts exciting to be around, they need to be careful that their natural tendency to action does not bring them undone when making important financial decisions.
- Extraverts often enjoy the cut and thrust of debate. Consequently, they can be vulnerable to the exciting, lively sales talk of entrepreneurs with 'get rich quick' schemes. This fact is probably behind the old saying, 'The easiest person to sell to is a salesperson'. Therefore, Extraverts need to remind themselves that in retirement they will not have the earning capacity to recover from heavy losses resulting from hastily considered financial decisions.

If you are an Introvert (I)

- Introverts lean towards activities that require quiet involvement and will often enjoy participating in projects that require prolonged, focused attention.
- Introverts prefer to communicate on a one-to-one basis, or in small groups of people that they know well. Given the choice, some Introverts may prefer that communication be written rather than oral.
- Introverts are less likely than Extraverts to react quickly, or to rush into decisions. However, they need to ensure that they do not allow their tendency to think before they act freeze them into inaction.

If you are of the Sensing (S) preference

- Those with the Sensing preference will usually prefer to become involved in activities that are practical, and which have measurable, observable outcomes.
- Sensing people usually prefer to use the skills they have already developed than to learn new ones. It is therefore likely that they will prefer activities where they use skills that were acquired before they retired.

If you are an Intuitive (N)

- When looking for activities, Intuitives should consider including study or short courses. This is because they gain pleasure from acquiring new skills or knowledge.
- Intuitives' use of imagination and insight will often act as a catalyst for constructive discussion among other members of groups such as committees.

If you are of the Thinking (T) preference

- When people with the Thinking preference are seeking activities, they may be more comfortable in roles where they need to apply logic rather than dealing with the emotional problems of others.
- Where committee work is involved, the tough-mindedness of those with the Thinking preference will be important. However, they need to be careful that they do not react too impersonally, thereby hurting others' feelings in the process.
- When it comes to financial decisions, those with the Thinking preference will be more likely to apply cool, analytical solutions to decision-making. While this is a valuable approach when it comes to financial decision-making, they will also need to check that their partner is happy with the proposed outcomes.

If you are of the Feeling (F) preference

- When those with the Feeling preference are making important decisions, they will tend to be influenced more by their values than by the logical outcome that the cold, hard facts may suggest.
- Because of their desire to please others, those with the Feeling preference may find it difficult to break bad news, or to provide critical opinions to others even when it is required.

If you are of the Planned Schedule (PS) preference

- Those with the PS preference will usually prefer activities that involve a reasonably high level of structure.
- Once a plan of action is decided, those with the PS preference usually dislike changes along the way, preferring to stick to their original plan.
- In committees, PS people are likely to focus on the milestone dates that tasks need to be completed by, because they are driven by their need to bring projects to closure.

If you are of the Flexible Schedule (FS) preference

- Those with a FS preference will most likely enjoy activities involving change or flexibility from rigid schedules.
- Where it is important that an activity or project is completed on time, those with the FS preference will need to be careful that they do not keep postponing the completion of tasks because they 'need more information'.
- Because they like change, those with the Flexible Schedule preference will need to ensure that the activities they seek do not involve too much routine or repetition.

'Mapping' personality preferences to improve performance

Mapping involves identifying all the actions that comprise a task and then checking them off against your own personality preferences. Where you find that a task does not match your particular preferences, you simply make a note to take special care during this phase of your activity. For example, if you are an Intuitive (N) but find that the task requires attention to fine detail, you can simply make a conscious decision to focus carefully during this phase of the task.

Below is a process for mapping your preferences against the tasks you have to complete, or the decisions you need to make.

Mapping your personality preferences against a task you need to complete

1. Ensure you are familiar with the descriptions of your personality preferences listed earlier in this chapter. [Note: You may wish to complete a formal preference inventory, such as the Myers-Briggs Type Indicator (MBTI), with a qualified practitioner.]
2. Ask yourself, 'What personality attributes does this task or decision seem to require?'
   (i) Does the task or decision require quiet concentration for prolonged periods of time (Introverting behaviour), or does it need someone to promote concepts/ideas to others or to interact with groups of people (Extraverting behaviour)?
   (ii) Does the task or decision require accuracy and attention to fine detail (Sensing behaviour), or does it require a vision of how to do things differently from the way they have been done in the past (Intuitive behaviour)?
   (iii) Does the task or decision require an objective, logical approach, or the implementation of tough decisions

(Thinking behaviour), or does it require you to focus on the personal impacts of decisions on others (Feeling behaviour)?

(iv) Does the task or decision require spontaneous behaviour with many changes and new inputs along the way (Flexible Planning behaviour), or does it require working to a detailed plan or schedule where meeting agreed timetables is important (Planned Schedule behaviour)?

3. Having identified and listed the personality attributes required to successfully perform the task, ask yourself, 'Which of these attributes are *not* typically found among my personality preferences?' Review the personality variables described earlier and make a list of the *less* preferred areas of your personality (those of the opposite preferences to yours), which are important to successfully performing the task or making the decision.
4. Finally, now that you have identified the personality attributes that were *not* found among your personality preferences, make a list of them and keep them close by during the task or decision-making process. If, for example, you need to focus for long periods by yourself but, as an Extravert prefer to mix with others, say to yourself, 'It is important that I remain focused during this time. Therefore, while I would dearly like to get up and engage people in conversation, I will use self-discipline and remain quietly focused for as long as I need to be to complete the task.'

   Similarly, if you are an Intuitive and the task requires attention to detail, say to yourself, 'While my tendency is to skim pages looking for broad trends, I will discipline myself to check each figure carefully. I *can* do this even if I find it irksome!'

How your personality and that of your partner affects your relationship

In the following section, we will look at relationship issues that may arise due to the interaction of particular personality styles. Understanding where your respective personalities are aligned, and where they differ, will allow you to better appreciate the attributes you share in common. Conversely, through insight and understanding you are more likely to be understanding of your partner's personality preferences where they differ from, or clash with, your own.

Aspects of our personality that complement each other	Aspects of our personalities that require monitoring
We both identify with the Extraversion (E) preference	
• We both enjoy socialising and entertaining. • We find it easy to discuss issues that are concerning us. • We like to keep busy by having a number of activities on the go at once.	• Because we both like talking and interacting, we may not listen carefully enough to each other. • Our levels of activity are high but we need to ensure that we share some activities so that we spend enough time together. • We need to ensure that in accommodating each other's need for action, we set aside some time for individual reflection and thought.

Aspects of our personality that complement each other	Aspects of our personalities that require monitoring
One of us identifies with the Extraversion (E) preference and the other with the Introversion (I) preference	
• The outgoing E takes pressure off the I to 'perform' at social occasions. • The I enjoys listening to the E, who in turn enjoys talking. • The E's enthusiastic, outgoing personality is balanced by the I's quieter personality.	• When we are both suffering from stress, the I needs peace and solitude to recover, while the E may prefer to surround themselves with people. • When we have a major problem to solve together, the E may want to discuss it with the I so that they can work out the problem together. However, the I may prefer to solve the problem alone first and then discuss the solution. • The I wants more privacy and time alone than the E, who may have difficulty in understanding this need for solitude and contemplation.
We both identify with the Introversion (I) preference	
• We enjoy quiet times alone together or with small groups of people who we know well. • We understand each other's need for privacy and time alone. • We can be in the same room together for hours without feeling the need to keep a conversation going, or to attend to each other.	• We find that providing negative feedback to each other is difficult. This may mean that we bottle up issues for too long until they blow out of proportion. • Because we do not discuss important issues as often as we should, we may wrongly assume that our actions meet with our partner's approval. • We risk becoming too isolated from others due to our contentment with our own company.

Aspects of our personality that complement each other	Aspects of our personalities that require monitoring
We both identify with the Sensing (S) preference	
• We do not overcomplicate our lives with mess and clutter. • We live in the here and now and do not waste time dreaming of a better future. • We do not cause ourselves stress through poor record keeping, for example, by forgetting to pay bills.	• We may neglect to plan sufficiently for the future. • We may not try new ideas to solve recurring problems differently, thus limiting our ability to solve problems and move forward. • We may miss the opportunity to learn new skills due to our reliance on the methods we have used for years.
One of us identifies with the Sensing (S) preference and the other identifies with the Intuitive (N) preference	
• The S is good at putting the N's ideas into action. • The S attends to important matters in the here and now, while the N thinks about new ideas for the future. • The N can help the S to appreciate abstract concepts, while the S can help the N keep their feet on the ground.	• The N may irritate the S through their inattention to detail. • The S may irritate the N through insisting that they keep everything tidy. • When it comes to designing or decorating a residence, the S may focus on a practical design while the N may prefer a radical, less practical design.
We both identify with the Intuitive (N) preference	
• We welcome change and new ways of doing things. • We find it easy to communicate with each other using theory and abstract concepts.	• We may become stressed because we have too much going on in our lives at once. • While we are good at generating ideas, we do not always bring them to fruition. • We may neglect the practical essentials of life such as maintaining the house and car, and organising the orderly payment of bills.

Aspects of our personality that complement each other	Aspects of our personalities that require monitoring
We both identify with the Thinking (T) preference	
• We rarely offend each other because of poor communication. • We use logic to solve problems and do not become over-emotional.	• We may forget to say 'I love you'. • We may find it difficult to attend to people's needs when they are visibly distressed. • We may have difficulty in showing our emotions.
One of identifies with the Feeling (F) preference and the other identifies with the Thinking (T) preference	
• The T finds it easier to be tough with people where this is required, and the F is more inclined to offer comfort and sympathy to those in distress. • The feelings and emotions of the F are balanced by the T's logical approach. • We complement each other with our objective (T) and subjective (F) views of the world.	• When we are arguing, the T may offend the F with their cool, dispassionate logic. • The F wants peace and harmony while the T wants to resolve the problem. • Our public displays of intimacy are different, with the F being more demonstrable than the T.
We both identify with the Feeling (F) preference	
• We are both peacemakers and enjoy a harmonious relationship. • We consider each other's feelings and discuss issues to ensure that we both agree. • We genuinely like people.	• We may overreact to personal criticism. • We may neglect our individual needs in our desire to please our partner. • We have trouble resolving conflict due to our strong need to please others and to maintain harmony.

Aspects of our personality that complement each other	Aspects of our personalities that require monitoring
We both identify with the Planned Schedule (PS) preference	
• We reach decisions quickly. • We are both well organised and attend to our responsibilities with minimum fuss or procrastination. • We are both clear regarding the respective roles and responsibilities in our relationship.	• Because we are so task-oriented we may leave too little time to relax and indulge ourselves. • Our need for plans and organisation may result in clashes because we both have strong convictions about how things should be done. • Because we both value 'closure' we may rush into important decisions without sufficient information to allow for an informed choice.
One of us identifies with the Planned Schedule (PS) preference and the other with the Flexible Schedule (FS) preference	
• Our life is balanced between work and play. • Our life is balanced between plans, structure and order, and spontaneous fun.	• The PS may see the FS as too fun-loving and the FS may see the PS as too serious. • We arrive at decisions differently because the PS desires closure and the FS wants to delay closure to gain more information. • Household maintenance is important to the PS and is avoided by the FS.
We both identify with the Flexible Schedule (FS) preference	
• We enjoy change in our lives. • We do not tie each other down with rigid schedules. • We both enjoy fun times and ensure they form an important part of our lives.	• We may find that our house and car are poorly maintained. • Important bills may be neglected until they have passed their due date. • Lack of order in our lives may bring unnecessary stress.

SUMMARY:

In this chapter we . . .

- Described a model of personality based on the work of Carl Jung.
- Examined ways of applying knowledge of our personality to aspects of our life in retirement.
- Learned how to 'map' our personality preferences against tasks we need to complete.
- Learned how to optimise our relationship with our partner by understanding each other's personality preferences.

CHECKLIST

- ☐ I have read the descriptions of the four sub-scales of personality preferences described and understand how each differs from its opposite preference, for example, Extraversion versus Introversion.
- ☐ I understand that I can access attributes of my opposite 'letter' because they represent my *preferences*, not my skills.
- ☐ I have read the information on each sub-scale regarding its relevance to my retirement activities and pastimes.
- ☐ I understand how to map my personality preferences to perform better during important tasks or decisions.
- ☐ I know where the personality preferences of my partner and I complement each other, and which areas we need to monitor.

CHAPTER TWELVE

Cross-skilling in relationships

AIMS OF THIS CHAPTER

- To examine the need for partners to cross-skill.
- To learn what participants on the *Retire 200* project reported about being over-reliant on one partner.
- To identify key areas in which both partners should be competent.

The argument for cross-skilling

Research from the participants of *Retire 200* indicates that it is important for both partners in a relationship to be competent to perform the full range of duties that they manage collectively. Apart from issues relating to the fair distribution of responsibilities, it is important for both partners to know how to perform each other's roles for the following reasons:

- A partner can become ill, or unable to perform heavy work due to complaints such as arthritis.
- A partner may pass away.
- The relationship may end.

Clearly, any one of the above scenarios is associated with significant stress. Acquiring a new skill when also suffering from stress or grief makes the learning process all that more difficult, particularly when the skill is far removed from your usual repertoire.

What are the outcomes of not cross-skilling? Here are a few examples:

- Not knowing that it is important to check the temperature gauge in the car could result in a ruined engine costing several thousand dollars to replace.
- Not knowing that it is important to clean the lint filter on the clothes dryer could result in your house burning down.
- Not understanding the basic workings of your investment portfolio could result in poor, costly decisions.

'Teach your husband to cook and wash so you can go out and do what you want!'

The *Retire 200* participant quoted on the previous page had raised a large family in an older-style traditional household. Her husband's cooking skills were limited to the occasional weekend barbecue and he had never used the washing machine.

'When my wife left me it came out of the blue. I didn't even know how to cook and found myself going across the road each day to the takeaway food shop and living on fried dim sims, and chicken and chips. I spent a fortune on dry cleaning because I didn't know how to iron a shirt. I think it was the food, and the stress of the break-up, that finally made me so ill.'

The above man had moved as a young man from home where his mother had done all of his cooking and ironing, straight into a marriage where his wife continued these roles. When his wife left him a month before he retired, he could not deal with the basics of cooking, or washing and ironing his clothes. Consequently, he relied on takeaway food for nearly a year. He would probably still be doing so had not an old mate, horrified by his friend's helplessness, intervened and taught him the basics of cooking and ironing. (Once he had learned the basics of cooking, he became somewhat of a cooking enthusiast. When I spoke with him, he was partway through a course on Chinese cooking and was loving every moment of it!)

'I was hospitalised for seven weeks and could not drive the car for another two months. During that time, my wife had not known to check the pressure in the tyres. When I finally got around to it, three tyres were okay but one of the back tyres was practically flat.'

It is bad enough for someone to eat takeaway food because they cannot cook. However, in the above example the driver could have ended up in a serious accident.

'Sometimes she fires up the lawnmower while I prepare the evening meal or put a load of washing through.'

These husband-and-wife participants on the *Retire 200* research had worked in demanding jobs for most of their lives, and owned a substantial home on a large block of land. When asked why they had cross-skilled, the husband indicated that they had initially started cross-skilling to take the load off each other when one of them was going through a particularly stressful time at work. After they retired, they felt secure knowing that if one of them became ill or died, the other could still perform the essential functions of running the house and attending to responsibilities such as managing their investment portfolio.

'Some married women depend on their husbands too much – for example, some don't know how to use Internet banking to pay bills . . .'

This woman described how her husband had become very ill and could not perform the basic roles he had looked after all of their married life. She then found herself trying to learn new skills at this most stressful time in her life.

Cross-skilling

Many of the following points were identified by those on the *Retire 200* program as areas in which both partners should be competent. You may think of more to add.

Area of expertise	Partner A (✓)	Partner B (✓)
MOTOR VEHICLES		
Knowing what the car's tyre pressure should be		
Knowing how to check the tyre pressure		
Knowing how to inflate/deflate tyres to the correct pressure		
Knowing how to check the car's oil and coolant		
Knowing how to top up the car's oil and coolant (including windscreen washers)		
Knowing what fuel the car takes (petrol, diesel, LP gas)		
Knowing how to fill the car with fuel		
Knowing what the gauges on the car's instrument panel mean and why it is necessary to keep a regular eye on them		
Knowing to listen for unusual noises coming from the car and to immediately have them checked out by a mechanic		
Knowing to have the car serviced according to the recommended maintenance schedule		
LAWN MOWERS		
Knowing how to start and stop the mower		
Knowing what fuel the mower takes (petrol or two stroke)		

Area of expertise	Partner A (✓)	Partner B (✓)
Knowing how to check the oil if it is a four-stroke petrol mower		
Knowing how to check the blades		
Knowing to stop the mower before putting hands or feet near it or when emptying and replacing the grass catcher		
Knowing to wear protective eye/ear/foot wear when mowing		
Knowing how often to get the mower serviced		
SHOPPING – COOKING		
Knowing how to purchase the right food to ensure a healthy, balanced diet		
Knowing how to buy and store food to maintain freshness and avoid waste		
Knowing how to cook basic food items using methods such as steaming, roasting, grilling		
Knowing how to use the basic functions of conventional and microwave ovens		
Knowing how to clean conventional and microwave ovens		
WASHING/CLEANING		
Knowing what utensils must not be put in a dishwasher and what must be put on the top shelf only		

Area of expertise	Partner A (✓)	Partner B (✓)
Knowing how to use a clothes washing machine		
Knowing how to use a clothes dryer		
Knowing what clothes should and should not be put in washing machines and dryers		
Knowing how to clean the filters of dishwashers, washing machines, clothes dryers (dirty lint filters in clothes dryers are a major cause of house fires)		
Knowing what solvents and cleaners can and cannot be used on the various surfaces around the house (benches, tiles, marble, wood, paint, plastic, leather, cork tiles etc.)		
Knowing how to use an iron – set correct temperature, fill with water		
Knowing how to iron clothes		
USING APPLIANCES		
Knowing how to set the time clocks on all time-based appliances – DVD players, microwaves, stoves, clocks, bedside radios etc.		
Know how to access the basic information stored on your home computer		
Knowing how to use the basic functions of all electronic equipment in the home – radios, CDs, TVs, vacuum cleaners etc.		
Knowing when and how to change vacuum cleaner bags		

Area of expertise	Partner A (✓)	Partner B (✓)
Knowing how to test the batteries in the smoke detector(s)		
Knowing when and how to change the batteries in appliances such as smoke detectors, remote controls, radios, clocks etc.		
FINANCES		
Knowing how to manage your budget		
Having a system for paying bills and filing receipts		
Knowing how to complete your tax return or at least what records to maintain for your tax accountant		
Understanding your share portfolio and how to best use the services of your stockbroker or financial adviser		
Knowing how to access special benefits that are due to you (rebates, discounts relating to council rates, water, electricity, public transport etc.)		
Knowing what your social service entitlements are and how to access them		
Knowing how to put into action advice provided by your financial adviser		
MISCELLANEOUS		
Knowing the range of council services that may be available, for example, moving heavy furniture		
Having a list of reliable tradespeople		

SUMMARY:

In this chapter we . . .

- Identified reasons for cross-skilling within relationships.
- Identified a range of skills in which both partners should be competent.

CHECKLIST

- ☐ I understand why it is important for both partners to be competent across the range of tasks and responsibilities.
- ☐ We have examined the list of competencies and will begin to cross-skill where we find individual competency gaps.

SECTION FIVE

Managing money and avoiding traps

It may appear at first glance that a chapter on financial matters is out of place in a book dealing largely with lifestyle and psychological issues. However, the findings of the *Retire 200* program left little doubt that one of the most powerful factors influencing retirement-based anxiety, depression or stress related to being totally dependent on a government pension.

By the time most people pick up this book, their retirement will probably be either well under way or just around the corner. Consequently, this next chapter does not address the wealth-creation strategies typically found in books on superannuation or retirement planning. Rather, it is included to suggest that people seek expert advice to maximise existing financial circumstances, and to alert readers to some of the expensive traps highlighted by those who took part in the *Retire 200* research program.

CHAPTER THIRTEEN

Guarding your financial health

AIMS OF THIS CHAPTER

- To examine feedback relating to financial matters from participants of the *Retire 200* program.
- To identify a number of costly financial mistakes that can affect your life savings.
- To identify criteria for use when seeking professional financial advice.
- To provide a format for calculating weekly, monthly and yearly costs of living.

'In retirement you need twice as much money and half the clothes'

The *Retire 200* research indicated that financial matters – and, in particular, financial independence – rated among the top factors that influenced wellbeing. Those people who were not financially independent tended to experience higher levels of anxiety, stress and depression than those who were.

Note: 'financially independent' meant not depending solely *on government pensions for income – that is, having at least some income from other sources such as superannuation or personal investments.*

As the laws and regulations governing superannuation, retirement income streams and social security change so frequently, it is impossible for a book to provide other than very general information. Moreover, individual circumstances vary so widely that those seeking the answers to their retirement-related financial questions are wise to consult directly with a qualified, trusted financial adviser or other relevant professional.

Feedback from participants of the *Retire 200* program

Here are some of the observations of the participants in *Retire 200.* Most of these people held strong views about superannuation, government pensions, and how to manage their money. They were anxious to pass on these views for the benefit of others.

1. Living within your income

Those participants on the *Retire 200* program who were financially independent typically placed more importance on the security of their income than on the income they received. As more than one participant said, 'I like to sleep at night!'

Usually, the more conscious a person was of their income security, the more likely they were to have taken an active interest in the accumulation of their retirement savings. Even where the majority of their retirement wealth accumulation was funded by superannuation, security-conscious people could usually describe in some detail the investment portfolios that had comprised their superannuation plan.

At the collection end of the superannuation savings years, security-conscious retirees were also more likely than others to have both short-term budgets (for example, weekly living expenses) and medium-term budgets (annual holidays, car registration). It seems that those who had taken an active personal interest in accumulating wealth over their working life were also the most interested in managing it well during their retirement years.

Here are some of their observations:

'Live within your means. Don't worry about others' ideas like always having the latest car. Don't have silly expectations.'

'You need enough money to be comfortable.'

'Financial security is important – you don't need a lot but you need to be comfortable.'

'Make sure that you have enough money to support your interests.'

The core message appears to be, 'Look at your situation honestly and then resolve to live within your means.'

2. Getting the right advice

Younger retirees (aged fifty-five to sixty) were more likely than their older counterparts to have sought advice from a financial adviser. Older retirees appeared to be more suspicious of financial advisers, preferring to manage their own finances or to use an accountant. These days, qualifications for financial advisers, such as the Diploma in Financial Planning (DFP), and the existence of regulators such as the Australian Securities and Investments Commission (ASIC) provide a higher degree of comfort for people seeking advice. However, as in any industry or profession, there are still those people providing advice that reflects their own interests rather than the welfare of their clients.

When selecting a financial adviser, most participants indicated that they wanted someone who was competent and who understood their needs and circumstances. Importantly, they wanted to feel at ease with their adviser due to the private financial matters they would need to disclose to them (criteria to consider when selecting a financial adviser are discussed later in this chapter).

'Have a budget that you stick to – this will reduce stress over money worries.'

'Get a good accountant or financial adviser to explain investments to you.'

'Plan your finances before and after retiring.'

'Seek financial advice.'

3. It's never too late

'If you need money, go out and make some.'

The above comment came from the *Retire 200* participant who had set up a small business selling products out of the boot of his car at markets (see Chapter One on Purposeful Activities). He and a number of other participants demonstrated that it is possible to generate income in retirement without taking large financial risks, without necessarily investing large sums of money, and without having special qualifications or experience.

Note: it is often possible for retirees to obtain part-time or casual employment without having to pay much tax. However, like most financial matters, always check with the relevant authorities such as Centrelink and the Australian Taxation Office to verify how such employment will affect your circumstances.

4. Anxiety, depression and stress due to a lack of financial security

We have discussed previously that the link between the psychological problems of anxiety, depression and stress, and having insufficient financial resources was a significant finding in the research. In particular, stress caused by money worries was of great concern to many who regarded it as detrimental to their health. Even when financial problems were not an issue, most people could cite examples of friends or relatives who were 'doing it tough'.

'Go and have your finances checked out to have a stress-free retirement.'

'Understand your financial needs. Some people get very stressed over finances.'

'You need to have enough money to be worry free.'

'Plan your money details so that you do not have financial worries.'

'Beware of taking a lump sum. If you do not have a business mind you may invest in a catastrophe and lose the lot. I have seen many lose their money that way.'

'Your finances need to be sound for (i) security, and (ii) to be independent.'

'Financial stability and your health are important.'

To summarise, those who felt confident that their financial circumstances were secure were in better emotional shape than those who were constantly worried about money.

5. Living solely on the age pension

Managing solely on the age pension challenged the ingenuity and creativity of most recipients. The very few who appeared to get by unscathed on the pension either had very simple, basic needs due to their lifestyle preferences, or they were receiving financial assistance from their family or elsewhere. Some pensioners' adult children supplemented their parents' income by funding specific financial outgoings such as car registration or hospital benefits. For the majority of those on the age pension, however, life was difficult, with few dollars available for non-essential commodities.

'You must be financially secure, even if you're on the pension.'

'I'm on the pension and money dominates my life – I am always worried about money.'

'Having enough money is number two after health. Surviving on the pension is terrible – there is no money for the pleasures of life.'

'When you are both on the pension you need to be inter-accountable re: spending because money is very scarce. It is galling to have to justify to each other when you want to spend a few cents – you feel like a child again!'

'You need money to pay for things that you are accustomed to.'

6. Debts after retirement

By far the worst off financially were those people who had arrived at retirement still in debt and who were on the pension. Trying to manage on a low income while still paying off a mortgage or other debt drove many to despair.

The main causes of debt after retirement were:

- Debts carried over from a failed business.
- Refinanced home loans following a divorce late in life.
- Inappropriate credit card usage – this was usually caused by one or both partners' entrenched credit card spending habits that were not modified even after their earning power to repay card debits had diminished.
- Acting as a loan guarantor for a friend or relative who then defaulted on the loan.
- Gambling – this is an ever-growing problem, with high volumes of poker machines spread around the suburbs and rural areas.

'You need to be financially secure and must have NO debts. Money worries will affect your health.'

'Own your own home – it is essential that it is debt free. Have a secure income source.'

'You can't retire with debts. You can't afford to pay them back.'

'Don't have debts when you retire. Watch your credit card spending – get into the habit of not being a consumer.'

7. Active financial management

Interestingly, those participants who chose to become involved in the ongoing management of their retirement income tended to become *very* involved. For some of these people, the management of their income became a Purposeful Activity in itself. The first page of the morning paper to be read came from the financial section and many used software packages to track the performance of their investments.

Maintaining your financial health

For most of us, retirement signals the end of the wealth-accumulation phase funded through salaries or business income. It is now that the important business of maintaining our retirement savings begins, to ensure that they outlast us! This section of the chapter looks at a number of steps to consider for maintaining your financial health.

Your first steps

Before you seek advice from anyone, it is important to spend some time examining your financial needs and goals. You need to be clear about what services you want. Are you seeking advice about one particular investment, or do you want a full financial plan? Are you concerned about estate planning, that is, what happens to your money when you die? Naturally, a competent adviser will assist you to clarify these issues. However, in the first instance you should examine needs and goals before you consult your adviser. During this time you should also think about how you will control the discussion with the adviser. Always remember that it is your money and you should not just delegate *all* the responsibility for decision-making to an adviser.

Selecting a financial adviser

Seeking professional financial advice can be a good financial investment in itself, as there may be ways for you to improve the net income you derive from your investments. For example, a competent financial adviser may suggest that you restructure your financial affairs to legitimately minimise the tax for which you are presently liable.

The process you need to go through to find a good financial adviser is similar to that for finding a good dentist, doctor or vet. If you do not presently have a financial adviser, or you have one that you are not satisfied with, you may wish to consider taking the following steps:

- Ensure that the person you are intending to seek advice from holds the necessary qualifications. The Financial Planning Association (FPA) can provide you with the names of qualified financial advisers in your area.
- Ask your friends and relatives about financial advisers they have used and with whom they are happy. It is important to seek recommendations, because relying on obtaining names from the FPA is similar to asking the Australian Medical Association for the name of a doctor: both organisations will put you in touch with people who meet the requirements of their association. However, what they will not, and cannot, tell you is if the people they suggest are really any good at what they do, or whether they will suit you personally.
- Ask to see the adviser's licence or their authorisation to provide advice. Don't be too embarrassed to do this. The adviser will not resent this unless they have something to hide.
- Ask them if they have professional indemnity insurance and who their insurer is (if they do not have this insurance, do not deal with them).

- Ask the adviser if they provide a free initial session. Go and meet them so you can form an opinion of them.
- Ask them about their practice – see if they are proud of what they do.
- Ask them how long they have been in business.
- Ask them whether they have clients in similar financial situations to you.
- Ask what areas they can provide advice on, and whether they have a bias towards any products in particular.
- Ask them how they do their research – look for evidence of current journals and subscriptions to research services.
- As you speak with the adviser, try to build a picture of their expertise and integrity.
- Look at their office and staff – are they enthusiastic and professional?
- Most importantly, ask *yourself* whether you feel comfortable with them. You are the client – if you are not happy with them, leave.

What you should expect from a financial adviser

A competent financial adviser should include the following steps in their planning process with you:

- Gain an understanding of your lifestyle, feelings, preferences, objectives and existing financial plans.
- Find out what your tolerance for risk is through identifying your 'risk profile'. This simply means finding out how you feel about high-yield, high-risk investments versus lower-yield, lower-risk investments.
- Prepare the financial plan in writing.
- Conduct a session where the financial plan and recommendations are presented to you.

- Address issues beyond income, such as estate planning.
- Commence the implementation process where the strategies are put into action.
- Establish the need for regular reviews to ensure your plan stays up to date. These reviews need to be tailored to your situation. For some people, an annual review is recommended; for more complicated or volatile portfolios, reviews may even be quarterly.

What should a financial plan cost?

You should shop around, as fees can vary from adviser to adviser. Let them know approximately how much you have to invest and tell them that you need an estimate of the total charges to you. It is important to ask for a total amount because advisers may charge you in a number of ways, for example:

- rate per hour
- flat fee
- fee calculated on the amount of money that you invest with them
- commission based on the financial products you may purchase.

Do not forget that whatever the method of payment, you are paying for good advice. If you find a lower cost adviser, ensure that they are still capable of providing you with the quality of service you need.

What information will I need to divulge to my financial adviser?

Once you are dealing with your carefully selected adviser, you will need to provide all the information that you and the adviser regard as necessary to form an accurate picture. They will need to know where you are now financially, where you intend to go financially and when you wish to get there. Below is a list of the type of details you may have to provide:

- your assets
- your daily expenses
- your liabilities
- your present income
- your state of health
- your superannuation and insurance
- your tax liabilities
- your age and that of your partner
- if you are married and whether this is your first marriage
- your goals
- your concerns
- your plans and objectives requiring capital expenditure, for example, holidays
- your preference if becoming ill, for example, staying at home under care or moving to a nursing home
- your intentions for your money on your death.

How do I know if I have a good financial plan?

Does the plan provide all the information that you asked for? If the answer is *yes*, you are on the right track. However, you should also review the following points:

- Obviously the plan must be in writing. It should include information about what is being invested where, and why *this* plan suits your specific needs.
- Think about the process that your adviser went through when developing your plan. Did they ask you sufficiently detailed questions about your finances and your goals and preferences? Did they appear to be listening or did they act as if they already

'knew' what you needed? If they committed the unforgivable sin of commencing to sell a product without thoroughly examining your needs, dump them.

- Ensure that *you* have also been totally honest and forthcoming with information. Advisers cannot read your mind and they need to know all about your goals, present financial situation and tolerance for investment risk-taking.
- Do you understand what has been recommended and why it has been suggested as a solution for you? If not, keep asking questions until you do. It is the planner's responsibility to be able to clearly explain the details of a financial plan to even the most naive of investors.

Accessing pensioner concessions and senior's benefits

A retired friend decided on the spur of the moment to travel by train from the outer suburb he lives in to an outer suburb on the other side of town. Some weeks later, by accident, he discovered that he could have accessed concessions which would have reduced his fares to about one third of what he had paid.

It is worthwhile contacting relevant government departments, including the Australian Taxation Office and Centrelink, to discover what current literature they have about concessions or benefits based on age or income after retirement, even if you do not receive social security benefits. Your local council, retired people's organisations and clubs can also provide assistance. If you are not sure, ask – it does not cost you anything!

Avoiding scams, tricksters and desperados

Retired people have long been a popular target market for confidence tricksters. Paradoxically, it is the very need to preserve and maintain their precious retirement savings that leaves some people open to 'get rich quick' schemes.

Fortunately, there is a government organisation that can check the credentials of companies on your behalf: the Australian Securities and Investments Commission (ASIC) can be found at www.asic.gov.au. While they will not provide advice about the likely performance of a legitimate organisation, they can provide the following information:

- Whether the organisation you are considering investing in actually exists.
- If the organisation has a proper prospectus.
- If the organisation has the appropriate licence if it is running a managed investment scheme.
- If the adviser is licensed.

One of the reasons that otherwise intelligent people fall for the schemes of confidence tricksters is that often the investment or scheme appears credible in theory. Con men and women do their homework, and understand the desires of their 'market'. The proof of this is found in one of ASIC's reports, called *Jailhouse Shock*. In this scam a bankrupt lawyer (who was actually in gaol as he ran the scam) managed to extract over 1.4 million dollars from eight investors. The scheme centred on convincing the investors that there was a fortune to be made in Canadian Government Treasury Bonds. The crooked lawyer managed to con a former bank manager, a chartered accountant and a stockbroker.

Remember that, invariably, the higher the advertised return on your investment, the higher the risk, that is, the potential for you to lose your money.

Internet and telephone scams

Most people with basic computer and word-processing skills are capable of producing a document, complete with company logo, that appears to represent a bank, government department or other organisation. Having produced such a document, scammers will make bogus demands for late or unpaid fees, or the need to 'update' your personal details including your bank account number, your credit card details or your Personal Identification Number (PIN). The scammers who contact you by telephone demanding similar details can be just as convincing. Obviously, no reputable organisation will canvass you for any of these details over the telephone or via email.

Budgeting

- Seek advice from government agencies, and financial professionals, to determine if there is a better way to structure your assets and investments. If you are not presently receiving an age pension, there may be a way for you to access at least a part pension.
- Draw up a budget and monitor your spending to ensure that you are not letting money slip through your fingers.

The form below contains a breakdown of the types of expenses most of us face during the year. Completing a budget such as this can help you identify your outgoings and may even help you focus on areas where you could make some savings.

	$ per week	**$ per month**	**$ per year**
Food			
Alcohol/soft drinks			
Dinners/lunches out			

	$ per week	$ per month	$ per year
Groceries – all food items			
Anything else?			
SUBTOTAL			
Accommodation			
Building and contents insurance			
Electricity			
Gas			
Maintenance/repairs			
Mortgage payments/rent			
Municipal rates			
Telephone			
Water rates			
Anything else?			
SUBTOTAL			
Transportation			
Comprehensive insurance			
Driver's licence			
Fuel			
Lease or loan repayments			
Parking fees			
Public transport/taxis			
Registration and third party			
Service/maintenance costs			
Anything else?			
SUBTOTAL			
Health			
Dental expenses (net of benefits)			
Health insurances			
Medical expenses (net of benefits)			
Optical expenses (net of benefits)			

	$ per week	$ per month	$ per year
Pharmaceutical supplies			
Anything else?			
SUBTOTAL			
Personal			
Clothing/footwear			
Entertainment			
Fees			
Gifts			
Haircuts			
Holidays			
Life insurance			
Papers, books			
Recreation and hobbies			
Anything else?			
SUBTOTAL			
Miscellaneous			
Charities			
Pets/veterinary fees			
SUBTOTAL			
TOTAL			

To move or not to move

'Think carefully about relocating – don't make the final commitment straightaway – rent for six months first – you lose communication with family and friends, facilities such as hospitals. You find yourself in a different social environment, and a different social pecking order (you stand out!).'

'We moved from Sydney to Brisbane – it was great at first because we were able to buy a larger house with a pool and a view of the sea. However, we started missing our friends and family terribly and we then found that we could not afford to move back without dropping our standard of housing below what we had before we left.'

One of the most costly mistakes people can make in retirement is to move house without giving sufficient thought to the possible consequences. Sometimes the motivation to move is based on the desire to start a new life that is carefree and full of fun. Work is over, the family has grown up, the children are now independent, and the big 'holiday' is about to start. With thoughts like this in mind, it can be tempting to leave the old environment behind and start afresh in a new location.

If you move interstate, you will find removal costs are very high. These costs may double if you find that one or both of you cannot adjust to the new area and wishes to return to the old neighbourhood. A further complication arises when people have moved to a lower-cost area or state and then find that relocating to their old, more expensive neighbourhood is now beyond their financial reach.

The following 'fact-finding' questions were suggested by people on the *Retire 200* program, and from research into the risks associated with moving house after retirement. Therefore, before you move north, south, east or west, take the time to consider these points. Discuss them with your partner – make sure that *both* of you feel the same way, and that neither of you is under undue pressure from the other to move.

	Y	N
Is your extended family an important part of your social and emotional life? If so, will moving deny you sufficient access to them?		
Are you the type of person who values the company of old friends from the neighbourhood more than newer friends?		

	Y	N
Is the suggested move motivated by the desires of both partners, or is one driving the issue to live in a distant area where, say, the fishing is good?		
Will you seriously miss the memories, contacts and history of the house and area in which you presently live? Will the new house/area compensate sufficiently for the loss of these?		
How important is the familiarity of the area in which you presently live? Does this familiarity provide you with a sense of wellbeing and safety that you will miss?		
Is your sole reason for moving based on your inability to maintain your house or to live independently? If so, your local council may provide subsidised, or even free, assistance when you need to change a tap washer, install a new powerpoint, or lop a dangerous tree limb.		
Will the new area you are considering have the range of quality services that you may need as you get older?		
Is there reliable public transport, a good shopping centre, and a range of medical services nearby?		
Are there activities and clubs in the area that suit your needs?		
Are you being pressured to move because others are trying to tell you to do what *they* think is good for you?		
Have you considered renting interstate for a year and leasing your home out? At least in this way it is possible to come back to your old home in your old neighbourhood, if things do not turn out according to your expectations.		
Are you succumbing to Moving Mistake 1? *		
Are you succumbing to Moving Mistake 2? **		

* *Moving Mistake 1*: Moving to the town where you have enjoyed your holidays for the last twenty years. The problem with this decision is that you assume that the fun you previously experienced there will persist in retirement. Holidays are fun because they provide change from routine; however, if they *become* the routine, they may cease to amuse.

Holiday destinations are also usually associated with circumstances not able to be replicated in retirement. For example, the weather may not be as good in the off season and the regular dining out at restaurants, all of which contributed to your holiday fun, may not be sustainable in retirement.

** *Moving Mistake 2*: The very worst time to decide to move is during or immediately after a time of significant anxiety, depression or stress. As mentioned earlier, emotional issues arise when we are forced to retire against our will, or when we have lost a partner. Moving at these times can be tempting because it can signify a new beginning. However, for all the reasons mentioned above, the decision to move should be made carefully, calmly and for the right reasons.

Moving to a retirement village

The complexities of moving to a retirement village are such that the whole next chapter is devoted to this topic.

SUMMARY:

In this chapter we . . .

- Received feedback from participants of the *Retire 200* regarding their financial experiences in retirement.
- Identified reasons for, and methods of, selecting a financial adviser.
- Identified a number of the steps in the financial planning process.
- Listed points to consider when thinking about moving house.
- Identified a range of expenses we need to include in our budgets.

CHECKLIST

- ☐ I have read and considered the feedback from the *Retire 200* research.
- ☐ I have considered the need to use a competent financial adviser.
- ☐ I have a better understanding of the financial planning process.
- ☐ I will consider the issues raised about moving house if I decide to move at some time.
- ☐ I will spend time drawing up a budget to monitor my/our spending.

CHAPTER FOURTEEN

Retirement villages

AIMS OF THIS CHAPTER

- To examine the legal, financial and psychological implications of moving to a retirement village.
- To reinforce the need to seek expert legal and financial advice before signing agreements and contracts with retirement village operators.

What is a retirement village?

Retirement villages comprise complexes of residential units that are built on common land. They are regulated by acts of parliament in each of Australia's states and territories, and in New Zealand. They receive no government funding and may be owned and administered either by not-for-profit organisations or by commercial entities. Generally, eligible residents need to be fifty-five years or older and to have retired from full-time work.

What is *not* a retirement village?

1. RESIDENTIAL CARE FACILITIES

Residential care facilities are aged-care facilities, once referred to as nursing homes or hostels. They cater specifically for residents requiring low-level and high-level care. In Australia, entry requirements include an aged-care assessment stipulated by the *Commonwealth Aged Care Act 1997.*

2. RENTAL VILLAGES

Under this structure, residents rent units that have been built in the village by property developers or individuals. There are typically no in-going contributions, and rents are often based on a combination of the resident's government rent assistance allowance and a percentage of their age pension. Rental villages fall under the requirements of the *Residential Tenancies Act* in each Australian state or territory, and in New Zealand.

3. RESIDENTIAL PARKS/CARAVAN PARKS

In residential parks people rent a site and provide their own caravan or prefabricated unit.

What motivates people to join a retirement village?

Downsizing

Cleaning and maintaining a large four- or five-bedroom house with various living and dining areas may be viewed as a waste of time and effort when only one or two people live there.

Maintenance

Mowing lawns, tending to the garden, periodically painting the home, replacing floor coverings etc., are time consuming and expensive, particularly when outside contractors are required to do these tasks due to the resident's inability to do so themselves.

Reducing dependence on adult children and other family members

Busy adult children with children of their own are often 'time poor'. Knowing that their parents are safely living in a retirement village can reduce the guilt and stress they may feel when they need to get away to 'recharge their own batteries' at the end of a tough week. Some residents claim that they are pleased that living in a retirement village has the added benefit of reducing their children's stress.

Social contact

Fear of social isolation and loneliness, and the enjoyment gained from mixing with others, are reasons commonly cited by those who move to retirement villages.

Security

The need to feel secure, either from perceived increasing violence in the community or due to a possible health crisis in the future, may be met by living close to others in a retirement village community.

Declining mobility

The single-storey structures of retirement village units along with easy access to common areas make life easier for those who have reduced mobility.

Changing neighbourhood

The characteristics of the neighbourhood might have changed over time – nearby houses may have been replaced by high-rise dwellings, or the area may have become run down.

Close proximity to facilities

Having a swimming pool nearby, maintained gardens to walk past, and other facilities provided by the retirement village operators can make living in a village appealing.

Why do people decide *not* to join a retirement village?

Emotional attachment to the family home

The family home will often be filled with many happy memories. Children's parties, Christmas mornings opening presents, a wedding in the back garden, can make leaving the home an emotional wrench.

Investment considerations

In most cases the family home can be expected to increase in value over time. This factor is important to those people who wish to have more financial options in the latter years of their lives or who wish to maximise their estate for their adult children. The high exit fees (see explanation on page 281) specified in many retirement village contracts mean that the decision to live in a retirement village is often more to do with lifestyle than investment.

Independence

Many people place a high value on their independence and do not want to be tethered by contracts. They may also resent the need to adhere to the many rules and regulations associated with living in a retirement village.

Reduced privacy

Living in close proximity to others may mean that your activities, attitudes, and political and religious affiliations eventually become common knowledge.

Gardening

Maintaining a garden and taking regular trips to hardware stores and nurseries for supplies are enjoyable pastimes for keen gardeners who would be saddened to have to leave these activities.

Friends and family in the area

Leaving friends and family who live close by may be too painful if a suitable retirement village can only be found some distance away.

Pets

Retirement villages have one of three approaches to pets:

1. They are allowed subject to approval of the pet's behaviour or size.
2. Existing pets are allowed but may not be replaced when they pass away.
3. No pets are allowed.

If you have a pet and the retirement village you are considering has strict rules concerning the keeping of pets, you may decide it is better to not move there.

Hobbies

(a) Noise: the rules relating to 'excessive noise' form part of the contractual arrangements for nearly all retirement villages. Usually, any noise that can be heard from outside a resident's unit is problematic. Therefore, people whose hobbies involve the use of electric tools such as drop saws, drills and routers may run foul of the rules even if only one resident complains. Similarly, the playing of musical instruments may be impractical in such an environment.
(b) Lack of space: hobbies may also become impossible to practise where space such as a shed is not available.

Living among 'old' people

The thought of living in a community of people all over fifty-five years of age is not an attractive proposition for everyone. Some claim they find it depressing to be surrounded by senior citizens and feel that by residing in a retirement village they are somewhat removed from the mainstream of society. This is especially the case where there is also a residential aged-care facility built on the same property. The onset of conditions such as dementia is a common fear of senior citizens and being confronted daily by views of people experiencing such a tragic decline can be very unsettling.

Legal and financial complexity

If you are thinking of moving to a retirement village, you are advised to give careful thought to the legal, financial and psychological impacts of such a move. If you skimp on developing a solid grasp of these areas before you make a decision, you risk finding yourself financially committed to a lifestyle that you did not fully anticipate and which you simply do not enjoy.

The operators of retirement villages will, on request, send you written information about their particular village. The document you will usually receive is referred to as a Public Information Booklet (PIB). If you think that a quick read of this document is going to provide you with all your answers, think again. Typically, the PIB can be around 120 pages long and peppered with legal and industry jargon. While explanations of any jargon used will usually be found in a *Definitions and Interpretation* section of the document, those without a legal background may find the sheer volume of unfamiliar terms overwhelming.

To add further complications to the mix, retirement villages are controlled by separate acts of parliament in each state and territory of Australia and in New Zealand. These acts are amended from time to time or may be replaced by a new act of parliament. At the time of this book's publication, the various state and territory acts were as follows:

New South Wales: *Retirement Villages Act 1999*
Australian Capital Territory: *Retirement Villages Act 2012*
Northern Territory: *Retirement Villages Act 1995*
Queensland: *Retirement Villages Act 1999*
South Australia: *Retirement Villages Act 1987*
Tasmania: *Retirement Villages Act 2004*
Victoria: *Retirement Villages Act 1986*
Western Australia: *Retirement Villages Act 1992*
New Zealand: *Retirement Villages Act 2003*.

Types of retirement village contracts

1. LONG-TERM LEASE OR LICENCE CONTRACT

Under these structures a fee referred to as an 'In-going contribution' is paid and in return residents receive a lease, or a licence, which allows them to live in one of the retirement village's units. The fee is essentially an interest-free loan to the retirement village.

In addition to signing a lease or licence contract, residents will be asked to sign a service agreement which lists the details of any General Service Fees and Personal Service Fees that may be payable. In most cases these fees are paid monthly or quarterly in advance.

General service fees

These fees are to provide for services such as gardening, general maintenance of the property, access to the village community centre, management and administration, any emergency call services that may be installed, use of the swimming pool, and a maintenance reserve fund or sinking fund. The fees may also provide for a village bus and shopping trips.

Personal services charges

These charges are on a user-pays basis and may include laundry, meals, cleaning and personal care. Personal services are not a feature of all retirement villages.

Exit fees

When a resident leaves a retirement village under the long-term lease or licence arrangement, the move will trigger an exit fee and other charges. The exit fee (sometimes called the 'departure fee' or 'deferred management fee') varies from village to village and even from unit to unit within the same village.

Retirement village operators will tell you that the exit fee has two purposes: first, it partly compensates the operator who had to bear the cost of building the village; second, it makes entry to the retirement village more affordable as part of the operator's costs are deferred until the resident leaves the village.

How exit fees are calculated

Participating option

The exit fee is calculated as a percentage (for example, 3 per cent annually) of the eventual sale price for each year that the resident stays in the village. This exit fee is then usually capped after a number of years. For example, a 3 per cent annual fee may be capped at 30 per cent after ten years. In this case, a resident's entitlement on leaving the village after ten years would be the sale price of the unit less 30 per cent. Hence, if the unit was sold for $580 000, 30 per cent of this amount would go to the retirement village and the resident's exit entitlement would be 70 per cent, i.e., $406 000 (less any other charges that may be due).

Non-participating option

In some circumstances the resident may not be able to afford to pay the full in-going contribution and may negotiate with the retirement village operator to pay a reduced amount. This arrangement is known as a non-participating option. There are two very important aspects of the non-participating option that should be carefully considered:

- The resident may not be entitled to share any capital gain when the property is eventually sold.
- When the unit is sold (in this example, after ten years), 30 per cent of the *sale price* is then calculated and may be deducted *not from the sale price*, as in the above participating option, but from the reduced amount the resident paid as an *in-going contribution.* As you can see from the tables on the following page, the resident's exit entitlement is significantly reduced under such a non-participating option. The non-participating resident who paid $60 000 less than the participating resident

as an in-going contribution then receives $230 000 less as an exit entitlement.

Example: Participating option – the resident pays the full in-going contribution

Full in-going contribution	$410 000
Resident pays the full in-going contribution	$410 000
Sale price after ten years	$580 000
30% is deducted from the sale price	$174 000
Resident's exit entitlement (before any other fees owing).	$406 000

Example: Non-participating option – the resident pays less than the full in-going contribution

Full in-going contribution	$410 000
Resident pays an negotiated amount which is less than the full in-going contribution usually required	$350 000
Sale price after ten years	$580 000
30% of the *sale price* is then deducted from the amount of the negotiated in-going contribution	$174 000
Resident's exit entitlement (before any other fees owing).	$176 000

Additional exit-related fees

On top of the exit fee, residents may be expected to pay a portion of the amount required to bring their unit up to a saleable condition. This can involve having the unit professionally cleaned, repainted, floor coverings replaced, and any damage repaired. Moreover, if the resident has installed additional equipment in the unit, such as a bidet, the retirement village operators may require that the resident pays the full cost of having it and its plumbing removed so that the bathroom area can be reinstated to its original condition.

In many cases residents will also be required to pay a portion of the cost incurred in finding someone to lease their unit, including obtaining a valuation, advertising, etc. There will also usually be charges known as 'termination administrative costs', which include solicitor's costs to prepare, execute and register the surrender of the lease. During the time that the unit remains vacant, the resident may be required to continue paying the service fees.

2. STRATA TITLE UNIT CONTRACT

In this scheme the resident pays the purchase price of the unit in a similar way they would if buying a unit in a block of units or flats. They then own the unit and become a member of the owners' corporation (sometimes called a body corporate). The process of buying in differs from normal strata unit contracts in that the resident must first be approved by the retirement village operator and will have to pay owners' corporation fees. If the resident is the first owner of a new unit, they may also be liable for GST.

When the unit is sold, the resident may be liable for some or all of the exit charges described above in the section on long-term lease or licence structures.

3. COMPANY TITLE

Few retirement villages operate under this structure. Here the resident purchases shares in a company which in turn owns the retirement village. A board of directors appointed by the shareholders manages the village and residents are required to comply with the company's constitution. When the resident leaves the village, they receive the sale price of their shares minus any exit fees.

4. UNIT TRUST

This structure is similar to the company title structure described above. The retirement village is owned by a trustee and the resident purchases a unit in the trust. If they leave the village, they are entitled to receive the sale amount of the unit less any exit fees.

5. PERIODIC TENANCY

This structure is sometimes used by not-for-profit organisations which manage community villages. There may be an in-going contribution, all or some of which may be refunded when the tenancy ceases. There is a lease but it has no fixed end date and operates from rental period to rental period.

Navigating the legal and financial minefield

Clearly, all the complexities surrounding the legal and financial aspects of moving to a retirement village are beyond the scope of this book. Prospective residents should speak with some residents of the retirement village they are considering, to get a feel for the social environment and the performance of the management team. While a general discussion with residents concerning the financial aspects of buying into the village could be helpful, it should be noted that not all residents will have the same contract conditions. Some may have contracts from an earlier time, or may have opted for a lower in-going contribution which is then later offset by a significantly reduced entitlement amount on leaving the village.

It is very important to seek quality legal advice and to have a solicitor examine all proposed contracts and agreements before you sign up. Even if you have a relationship with a solicitor who has performed conveyancing tasks for you in the past, or has prepared your wills and powers of attorney, they may not necessarily be the best person to wade through the details of retirement village contracts and service agreements. In the long run it may be less costly, and involve better-quality advice, if you go to a solicitor who is experienced in dealing with the area of retirement village contracts and who is familiar with the key areas that can be problematic. Each state and territory has a legal body which looks after the registration of lawyers and which also has a referral service for the public. These bodies are listed below and should be able to suggest solicitors specialising in retirement village contracts and service agreements:

Queensland Law Society
The Law Society of Western Australia
The Law Society of South Australia
The Law Society of Tasmania
The Law Society of New South Wales
The Law Institute of Victoria
Law Society Northern Territory
The Law Society of the ACT
New Zealand Law Society.

Current and future developments in contract clarity

In recent times, confusion experienced by some retirement village residents due to the complexity of their contracts, and the perception by some that they are being financially gouged by operators, has led to consumer groups and investigative journalists giving the topic prominent airing. It appears likely that the impetus for reform, and for the simplification of contracts, is only going to build in the foreseeable future, driven by increasing numbers of vocal baby-boomer retirees. The state-and-territory basis of the legislation controlling retirement villages suggests that any consistent nationwide reform will be patchy for some time.

Some social and psychological considerations

People entering a retirement village often cite the social benefits of living in a community as one of their prime motivators. Finding like-minded people with whom to associate can be an attractive proposition. However, the range of personality types, attitudes to life, differing political allegiances and differing cultural backgrounds can form a microcosm reflecting the diversity of society in general. It therefore stands to reason that while there will be people in the village whose company you enjoy, there will be others whose behaviour and attitudes may annoy or even offend you.

Given the close proximity of your neighbours, and the likelihood that you will meet each other regularly in the village's common areas, care needs to be exercised to ensure that unpleasant or hostile relationships do not develop. The last thing you need is to find that your life in the village is a stressful experience.

The saying 'An ounce of prevention is worth a pound of cure' is particularly apt when it is applied to maintaining good relationships. For example, if you lose patience and snap at a person who keeps trying to press their ideas or beliefs on you, you may find that the relationship will remain uncomfortable indefinitely. Using a strategy such as the 'fog'* technique can disarm the situation before it becomes a problem. The main benefit of the fog technique is that it allows you to withhold your agreement with another's views without either offending them or allowing yourself to be bullied into accepting their views just to shut them up.

**The 'fog' technique and other strategies for dealing with people are described in the section of this book titled 'Maintaining and Managing Relationships'. Here you will also discover strategies for resolving conflict and for asserting your rights.*

SUMMARY:

In this chapter we . . .

- Looked at the differences between Retirement Villages and residential care facilities.
- Looked at what motivates some people to move to a retirement village.
- Looked at some of the legal and financial aspects surrounding retirement village living.
- Looked at some examples of retirement village contracts and fee structures.
- Looked at some psychological and social aspects of living in a retirement village community.

CHECKLIST

- [ ] I understand what is, and what is not, a retirement village.
- [ ] I understand what motivates some people to join a retirement village and why some feel that such a life is not for them.
- [ ] Given the complexity of retirement village contracts, I understand the need to seek expert legal and financial advice before signing any contracts or service agreements.
- [ ] I understand the need to carefully manage relationships with other retirement village residents, the management, and the staff.

APPENDIX A

The 180° Relationship Check

Area	Terrible, ghastly	Needs to improve	Fair to average	Quite good	A saint
My general planning ability					
My money management					
My consideration for my partner's feelings					
My consideration for my partner's needs for autonomy and time alone					
My consideration for my partner's need for joint activities with me					

Area	Terrible, ghastly	Needs to improve	Fair to average	Quite good	A saint
The degree to which I accept responsibility for duties around the home					
The level of empathy I demonstrate when my partner is not well or is sad					
The degree to which I am prepared to attend an outing I will dislike but which I know my partner will enjoy					
The number of little things I do that say 'I love you'					
The level of respect I show for my partner's wishes and opinions					
The manner in which I speak to my partner at home					

Area	Terrible, ghastly	Needs to improve	Fair to average	Quite good	A saint
The manner in which I speak to my partner in public					
My preparedness to be welcoming and polite to friends of my partner who I do not like					
The effort I make to be pleasant when I am in a bad mood or upset					
The level of responsibility I take for communicating with our children and grandchildren					
My preparedness to answer the telephone when neither of us feels like it					
The level to which we share driving on a long trip					
My sense of humour					

Area	Terrible, ghastly	Needs to improve	Fair to average	Quite good	A saint
?					
?					
?					
?					
?					
?					
?					
?					

APPENDIX B

The Decision-making and Task-allocation (DMTA) matrix

List of responsibilities:

1. Deciding where to go for holidays
2. Setting our weekly/monthly budget
3. What colour to paint the house
4. Whether to move house or not
5. What price and style of house to purchase
6. Who looks after the tax returns
7. Who balances our budget
8. Who looks after our savings program
9. Who manages our investments
10. Who pays the bills
11. Who decides on purchases for maintenance, e.g., repairing versus buying a new hot water system
12. Who decides whether to buy new appliances, e.g., the latest TV
13. Who vacuums the house
14. Who cleans the toilets
15. Who decides what we will do today
16. Who decides who we will invite around for dinner
17. Who decides how we will maintain our health
18. YOU ADD SOME MORE

CELL A: 100% (These tasks/decisions are completely mine) e.g., *paying the bills* ....
CELL B: 50% – 50% (These tasks/decisions are discussed together and voted on) e.g., *where we go for holidays* ....

CELL C: 75% – 25% (These tasks/decisions are discussed together but if we do not agree my partner is the decision maker) e.g., *what colour to paint the lounge room*

....

....

....

....

....

....

....

....

CELL D: 75% – 25% (These tasks/decisions are discussed together but if we do not agree I am the decision maker) e.g., *what brand of television set to buy*

....

....

....

....

....

....

....

....

CELL E: 100% (These tasks/decisions are completely my partner's) e.g., *who looks after our tax returns*

....

....

....

....

....

....

....

....

Index

Michael Longhurst has worked as a consulting psychologist specialising in the development, delivery and management of learning and development programs both in his own practice and as the National Learning and Development Manager for a large Australian company. He is an internationally published author and leading authority in the area of adjustment to retirement. He has run regular seminars for retirees and people planning their retirement. His work is based on his psychological research with Australian retirees.